PERMISSION TO LEAD DIFFERENTLY

Eight Countries. One Awakening.
A New Way to Lead

C.M. ADOLPHE

Printed and bound in the United States of America
ISBN: 979-8-218-91774-6

DEDICATION

For Neil Sterrer, my sixth-grade teacher, who dared me in ways that were not typical for those days growing up in New York and gave me permission long before I learned to give it to myself.

He planted a seed—one that stayed with me, quietly growing, waiting for the moment it would finally blossom into a different way of leading.

LETTER TO THE READER

○

This book began with a question I didn't know I needed to ask: *What if strength isn't found in pushing harder… but in knowing when to pause?*

For most of my life, I lived in motion. Like many high performers, I believed excellence required constant output—another problem solved, another goal reached, another expectation met.

So I gave more.

More time.

More energy.

More of myself.

I prided myself on mental toughness—the ability to push through fatigue, pressure, and uncertainty without slowing down. For years, I believed that was the mark of strong leadership.

In many ways, it was also the lesson I was teaching my children.

I wanted them to understand discipline, perseverance, and the importance of striving for excellence. I wanted them to know that hard work matters and that resilience is a powerful asset in life.

In fact, I once had my son keep going after he broke his leg— believing he could push through the pain.

But somewhere along the way, I began to wonder if the lesson I was modeling was incomplete.

What happens when mental toughness becomes constant endurance?

When strength is measured only by how much we can push through?

Like many leaders, I kept going—pushing through exhaustion, doubt, and the quiet signals that something needed to change.

In our culture, stopping is rarely celebrated. Rest is often misunderstood. And stepping away—especially as a leader—can raise questions.

There are, of course, organizations that have begun to lead differently—where sustainability, reflection, and human capacity are part of the model, not exceptions to it.

But for many, that is not yet the norm.

I remember reviewing a résumé with a colleague for a senior executive role. One candidate had taken a two-month sabbatical. The reaction was immediate:

"I wonder what's wrong with this guy. Why would someone take two months off?"

The assumption was clear: Something must be wrong.

But I found myself thinking the opposite.

What if something was right?

What if the person who understands when to step back is the one who understands leadership most deeply?

That moment stayed with me.

Because the truth is, many of us are operating in a state of quiet burnout—giving endlessly to our careers, our organizations, our families, and the expectations we place upon ourselves.

Somewhere along the way, the human element gets lost.

We forget that we are not machines designed for constant output. We are human beings who require rest, reflection, and renewal.

This book was born from my decision to listen—to step away, to reset, and to rediscover clarity.

What began as a personal pause became a journey across countries, cultures, and quiet moments of reflection. It allowed me to reconnect with myself, with purpose, and with a deeper understanding of leadership—one shaped by a more evolved lens.

But more importantly, it gave me something I didn't realize I needed:

Permission.

Permission to slow down.

Permission to reflect.

Permission to step away in order to return stronger.

And perhaps most importantly, permission to redefine what strength truly looks like—for myself and for the next generation of leaders who are watching us.

My hope in sharing this story is that it offers that same permission to you.

Permission to recognize when you need to rest. Permission to honor the signals that tell you it's time to recharge. Permission to lead—and live—differently.

Because sometimes the most powerful thing we can do is pause long enough to remember who we are.

Thank you for allowing me the privilege of sharing this journey with you.

— C. M. Adolphe

CONTENTS

─── o ───

THE ARMOR AND THE ROAD

I didn't take this moment of pause or sabbatical, if you will, to travel for the sake of traveling. I paused because the weight of the armor I'd been wearing for decades had finally become too heavy.

Working toward perfection and excellence had been my shield. Achievement, my protection. In every boardroom, every negotiation, every impossible deadline, I believed that if I was flawless, I would be safe. It worked—until it didn't.

When I walked away, it wasn't a resignation from a role. It was a release. I wasn't searching for another role to serve, another ladder to climb. I was searching for my own voice—the one I'd buried under expectations, titles, and performance.

So, eight countries were mapped out for me. Not as a checklist, but as a pilgrimage. I decided that sixty was the right time to chart a different course. Sixty days for sixty years of life—a symbolic crossing into a different kind of freedom. I had decided that turning sixty wasn't an ending; it was an opening, the moment to choose a different course for my life.

Bali would teach me to let go. Japan, to move with intention. South Korea, to hold opposites in harmony. Tanzania would hand me a mirror, Ghana a new definition of pride, Egypt the courage to be seen, Switzerland the joy of surrendering control, and Colombia the audacity to live boldly. Each place chipped away at the armor, until there was nothing left between me and my truth. This is not a book about travel. It is a book about returning—to the self, to alignment, to the kind of leadership that doesn't require you to disappear behind a role.

I left wearing the armor. I came back without it. And everything—everything—changed.

This memoir does not begin at the beginning. It begins at a crossroads—the moment I stopped sprinting toward success and started asking what it had actually cost.

It begins at a place of reckoning, integration, and transformation.

It is about learning to lead with authenticity, to pause, to breathe, and to reclaim my life on terms meaningful to me.

Not to prove.

Not to protect.

But to serve. To align. To sustain.

This is the story of what remains.

And it is only the beginning.

CHAPTER 1

THE BREAKING POINT

> Sometimes the systems we serve
> show us exactly what we must
> refuse to become.

remember the quiet realization—not the kind that announces itself with drama, but the kind that settles in your body before it ever reaches your mind. I was looking around a table of decision-makers when it arrived, familiar and unmistakable. I had felt it before, in other rooms, at other tables. What was different this time wasn't a culture—it was my inability to keep pretending it fit.

The leadership environment I was witnessing wasn't new. It was simply no longer deniable. What was once considered tolerable, even navigable, suddenly felt misaligned with the kind of leader I truly was, the one I had buried beneath years of performance and conformity.

This is not the story of one organization, one individual, or one moment gone wrong. It's about a more universal reckoning—that subtle but undeniable shift when the values around you no longer reflect your own. When what's celebrated leans toward conformity over creativity, appearances over authenticity, and control over trust. I had been holding my breath for years inside systems that prized compliance more than curiosity. Eventually, the air ran out. The leader I had buried to survive demanded to breathe again.

On paper, everything looked like success.

Revenue was growing. New contracts were being won. Headcount was expanding. The metrics told a convincing story—one leadership was eager to celebrate. But paper has a way of telling only part of the story it's designed to tell.

I remember one quarterly review: A slide proudly showed a 40% increase in revenue over six months. What it didn't mention was that nearly half of that revenue came from a contract we weren't operationally prepared to deliver—one that would later require urgent remediation. Another slide celebrated a 20% jump in headcount, but it failed to mention that turnover in critical roles had quietly doubled.

The metrics weren't wrong—but they were incomplete.

What the dashboards didn't capture was the slow erosion beneath the surface—the burnout, the turnover, the lack of alignment, the ethical shortcuts designed as pragmatism. The quiet disengagement of people who once cared deeply. The slow normalization of urgency replacing strategy, and noise replacing visions. Growth was happening but grounding was not.

And in the silence between the bullet points, the truth was buried.

I wasn't the only one who felt it. Others would sense it too even if it was named differently. Closed-door conversations would pierce the air. It was felt in the steady stream of departures or in the hesitation of once confident leaders who had begun second-guessing instincts that used to guide them.

But while others adapted, I couldn't unknow what I knew.

Because while we were busy chasing growth, we had lost our grounding. The work no longer had meaning. Strategy had been replaced by noise. Vision by volume.

You can meet your goals and still lose your way. And we had.

I grew up in New York, the child of immigrant parents who believed excellence wasn't optional—it was survival. Achievement was our insurance policy. That mindset taught me how to deliver, endure, and succeed in spaces never designed with someone like me in mind. It sharpened my instincts. It built my capacity. And for a long time, it worked.

The culture I was in didn't reward excellence. It rewarded obedience. The ones who thrived weren't the most capable— they were the most compliant. Those who questioned the status quo, who challenged assumptions, were met with resistance. The unspoken rule was clear: Stay in your lane and you'll be fine.

And yet, instead of trust, I was met with scrutiny. Not because I wasn't delivering, but because I refused to disappear and adapt to a way of being that went against our responsibility.

I now understand why.

In environments where power is fragile, presence becomes a threat. I showed up—fully. I didn't hide behind titles. I spoke with clarity. I named what others avoided. I challenged assumptions not for the sake of disruption, but because I cared about outcomes. And that made some people uncomfortable.

I wasn't loud for the sake of being loud—but I was direct, confident, and unwilling to make myself smaller to ease the room. The performative parts of workplace culture never came naturally to me—the happy hours, the unspoken social choreography, the quiet negotiations of belonging. I didn't laugh simply to fit in or nod just to be accepted.

And because I didn't conform, I became an outsider. I didn't drink—not out of judgment, but out of choice. I didn't defer. I didn't ask for permission to lead—I just led. I delivered results, held teams together, raised the hard questions, and made hard things look possible. And in a culture that rewarded compliance over courage, that kind of leadership wasn't embraced. It was interrogated.

Because when systems rely on silence, assertiveness is mistaken for aggression. When power is built on control, clarity feels like defiance. And when you refuse to shrink, the room will often try to shrink you.

But I knew who I was. I still do. And that, ultimately, is what saved me.

I stayed longer than I should have. Like many women, I believed resilience was virtue. I believed I had to protect my team, prove my worth, earn my place. But what if the place was never designed to honor who I truly was?

That question—*what if the place was never designed to honor who I truly was?*—didn't arrive all at once. It unfolded slowly, through coaching, reflection, and a gradual unraveling of assumptions I had carried for decades. Assumptions about loyalty. About endurance. About what leadership was supposed to look like, and what it cost to practice it.

What if survival wasn't the goal anymore?

What if the goal was alignment—peace, even—with a deeper sense of knowing?

For most of my career, I had been comfortable working behind the scenes. I helped build companies, stabilize systems, and engineer growth quietly. I could adapt to almost any environment, translate chaos into order, and make progress without ever demanding visibility. I knew how to change the temperature of a room without drawing attention to myself.

But there is a difference between influence and belonging.

And over time, I realized I had mastered the former while quietly forfeiting the latter.

What I didn't fully understand at the time was what it was costing me internally. My outer life still functioned, but my inner system was misaligned. The body knows long before the mind is willing to admit when something is off. My health began to reflect the strain. My freedom of expression narrowed—not because I had nothing to say, but because saying it carried consequence. Parts of me went quiet to survive. What looked like endurance on the outside was actually dormancy on the inside. And something essential in me needed oxygen. It needed to be reanimated.

The voice inside me—the one I had learned to quiet in order to succeed—began to grow louder. It wasn't angry. It wasn't dramatic. It was steady, persistent, and clear. It asked better questions than I had been allowing myself to ask.

Why does urgency always outrank intention? Why does growth excuse misalignment? Why does leadership require so much performance and so little presence?

I entered ready to build something meaningful. And I did. But what began as a runway slowly became a trap. The pursuit of growth turned erratic, reactive, performative. Strategy gave way to impulse. Structure bowed to ego. There was always a next deal, a next push, a next fire to put out—but no shared pause to ask whether any of it made sense.

We began chasing opportunities not because they were aligned, but because they were available. Not because they strengthened our foundation, but because they fed momentum. Somewhere along the way, growth became the only metric that mattered, and the compass that once pointed toward purpose was quietly set aside.

When I raised concerns, I was met with polite confusion. As if asking questions disrupted the rhythm. As if logic slowed things down. As if reflection were a threat to progress.

Dissent didn't look like engagement—it looked like disloyalty.

And that's when the realization landed with full clarity: I hadn't lost who I was. But I had lost sight of who *we* were. The collective clarity that once anchored decisions had been replaced by urgency, ambition, and noise. The system no longer had the capacity—or the appetite—to listen.

I stopped trying to convince anyone.

Not out of resentment, but out of recognition.

There was a moment—quiet, almost ordinary—that clarified what I could no longer participate in. I was asked to persuade my team to speak positively, not honestly. Not to reflect, but to reinforce. I remember realizing that my work had shifted from building trust to managing perception. And that was a line I could no longer cross.

I began planning my exit quietly. Not just from a company, but from a mindset that told me I had to stay in misaligned spaces in order to be seen, valued, or validated. A mindset that equated sacrifice with significance and exhaustion with commitment.

What I was walking away from wasn't failure. It was performance without purpose.

At the same time, something else was taking shape. Not a job search. Not a title chase. But a return—to myself.

Eight countries called to me—places with rhythm, with roots, with reflection. I wasn't chasing healing; I was creating space for it. At first, I thought the choices were random. But as I moved from one to the next, I realized they weren't random at all. Life had arranged them like a quiet choreography, serving me the exact lessons I needed in the order I could receive them—a prescription for transformation written in geography and grace.

Because by then, I had seen how systems ration power. How leadership becomes performance. How the strongest voices are often the ones made smallest. And I was done shrinking.

That chapter of my life didn't break me. But it did bruise me. It didn't strip me of my power. It reminded me how sacred it is.

And so, I walked away. Not in bitterness. In truth. Because this life is too valuable to spend in rooms that ask you to disappear.

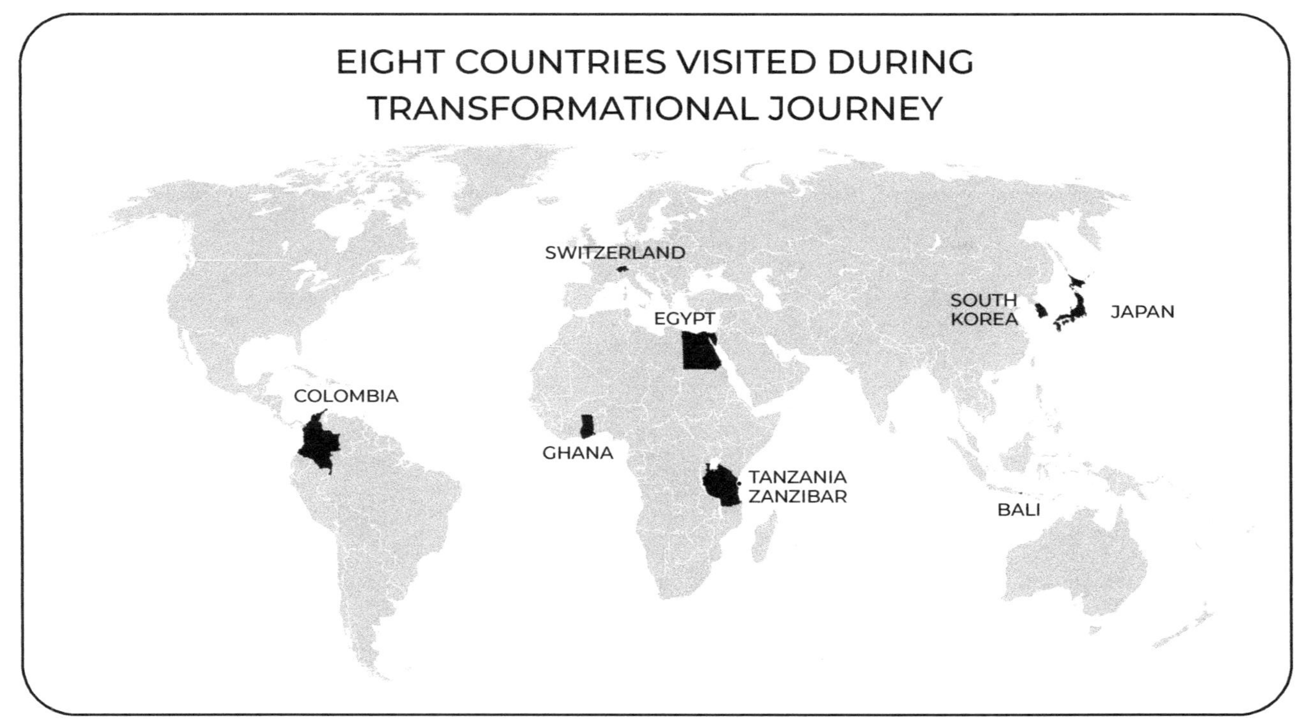
EIGHT COUNTRIES VISITED DURING TRANSFORMATIONAL JOURNEY
SWITZERLAND
SOUTH KOREA
JAPAN
EGYPT
COLOMBIA
GHANA
TANZANIA ZANZIBAR
BALI

CHAPTER 2

○

LETTING GO IN BALI

I wasn't trapped in the traditional sense. I had been a minority owner. A member of the C-suite. I understood the numbers. I had options on paper.

But leadership doesn't only bind you through contracts—it binds you through people, responsibility, and identity. Walking away wasn't a lack of courage. It was a confrontation with everything I believed leadership required me to carry.

I arrived in Bali carrying a lifetime of internalized discipline—the kind that teaches you to absorb tension without releasing it, to endure without signaling distress. Growing up, I learned early that seriousness was safety. I was told not to smile—that it made you seem unserious, unprepared, easy to dismiss.

So, I learned to manage my expression the way I managed everything else.

When I smiled or laughed, it was often at the exact moment I wanted to cry.

Joy became camouflage. Composure became currency. I learned how to keep moving while swallowing what hurt, how to succeed without softness, how to make the world comfortable even when I wasn't.

After walking away from a life built on urgency and expectation, I assumed I would feel lighter. Instead, what met me was space—wide, unstructured, unfamiliar. No meetings to anchor my day. No problems demanding resolution. No role to perform.

And in that openness, I began to notice how much I had been carrying—not outwardly, but inwardly.

Bali made no demands. Its rhythm was slow, ceremonial, soft around the edges. Each morning, I watched women place offerings on woven palm-leaf trays—incense, rice, petals—laid gently at thresholds and crossroads. They weren't performing. They were participating.

The air itself felt generous, asking nothing in return.

I tried to match the pace. But my mind had other plans.

Leadership had trained me to scan for what's missing— to anticipate risk, control outcomes, stay ahead of collapse. I thought I had left a way of being, but my nervous system hadn't caught up just yet. I was physically free, but still internally bracing myself. I was the strategist without a problem to solve.

The fixer with nothing left to fix. And it left me wondering: Who was I without the proving?

It became clear I needed more than rest. I needed recalibration.

The next day, I went to a water purification ceremony. For me, this wasn't a cultural excursion—it was a turning point. An emotional reset. A spiritual clearing I knew I needed if I was ever going to lead differently.

I began the morning at Tirta Empul Temple in Ubud, the sacred water temple fed by a natural spring where Balinese Hindus have come for more than a thousand years to cleanse the body, quiet the mind, and realign the spirit. They believe these waters were blessed by the god Vishnu, the protector and sustainer of life. Unlike guided rituals led by a healer, Tirta Empul is deeply self-directed—asking you to move through the waters on your own, step by step, with intention, attention, and presence.

There, I participated in Melukat, the traditional purification ritual. I joined the line of worshippers—families, elders, children, and travelers—all of us shoulder to shoulder, each carrying our own private prayers into the communal water. It was deeply humbling to feel my individual journey held inside a collective energy—everyone releasing, everyone surrendering, everyone seeking something just beyond language.

As the cool spring water poured over me from each spout, it felt less like being cleansed and more like being unclenched. Each pour washed away a layer of exhaustion, perfectionism, and unspoken weight I had carried for decades. And as I stepped from one fountain to the next, I realized that the work unfolding inside me was mine alone—guided not by a priest or healer, but by my own willingness to let go.

Tirta Empul reminded me that transformation isn't always witnessed. Sometimes the most powerful work is quiet, inward, and deeply self-led—held gently within the presence of others doing the same.

It marked a threshold—the moment I understood I could no longer lead from who I had been. I had to lead from who I was becoming.

"You cannot pour clean water from a vessel filled with residue. As a leader, you must first cleanse your own energy before guiding others."—*Author unknown*

Later in the week, after leaving Ubud, I transferred to Mandapa Reserve, a sanctuary tucked between rice fields and rain forest. The moment I arrived, I felt the shift. Mandapa was quiet in a way that didn't ask for silence but invited it. The air felt softer, the light warmer, the landscape layered with terraces of green that seemed to breathe in unison.

It was there, overlooking those rice fields, that I stepped into a multistage healing session in a serene yoga pavilion. The practitioner began with nadi shodhana—alternate nostril breathing. Inhale left. Exhale right. Switch. Repeat. Structured. Rhythmic. It reminded me of pacing a negotiation, of managing team energy in a boardroom—except this time, the team was me. It was an exercise intended to balance the nervous system and calm the mind.

As I settled into the breath, my thoughts softened. The noise began to quiet. This was preparation for chakra balancing—something I had once dismissed as mystical. But now I approached it as system alignment. After all, I'd spent decades optimizing financial frameworks, operational pipelines, and leadership models. Why not work on my own internal alignment?

The practitioner spoke of energy centers tied to power, voice, purpose, trust. As he placed stones and named each chakra, I recognized every theme from rooms I had once led. The solar plexus—personal power. The throat—communication. The root—security. I had felt the blockages in real time: the silencing, the second-guessing, the endless effort of proving my value in misaligned spaces. I realized that addressing the blockages is a necessary step because true healing, growth, and transformation cannot be obtained on a stable foundation if energy is stuck or misaligned. Energy cannot flow freely if it's not cleared to create space for growth or evolution.

Going back to my life, while I had continued to deliver outcomes, I had never paused to ask what that performance was costing me internally. I understood that this process was necessary.

That morning, I didn't experience transformation. I experienced integration.

The breath, the ritual, the silence—they didn't change me. They reminded me to bring all of me to the table again. Not just the strategist. Not just the executor. But the woman whose clarity doesn't require urgency to be valid.

In the days that followed, I walked slower. Ate slower. Sat longer. I noticed more—the intergenerational homes where elders, children, and parents lived under one roof, moving through life as a collective. It struck me how natural it felt here, how connection wasn't something scheduled but something simply lived. Back home, that kind of togetherness seems to have quietly faded, replaced by separation dressed up as independence. I took notice that the hotel staff met not just to plan, but to align. The unspoken grace in how hospitality was extended. There were no mission statements posted on the walls, yet the culture was palpable. The values weren't spoken; they were lived.

During my final days in Bali, I scheduled a meeting with a shaman—hesitantly. It felt almost taboo. I'd always believed that if we are still and attuned enough, we can chart our own course without an intermediary. Seeking out a shaman felt like admitting doubt in a compass I had spent a lifetime learning to trust.

Before that meeting, I visited Lempuyang Temple—the "Gate of Heaven." One of the oldest and holiest temples on the island, believed by Balinese Hindus to help anchor the island's spiritual energy. From a distance, the split stone towers framed Mount Agung, its summit veiled in clouds. Tourists lined up for the perfect mirrored photo, but I wasn't there for that. Standing before the gate, I felt myself on the threshold of something deeper—not between earth and sky, but between who I had been and who I was becoming.

The gate wasn't a portal to somewhere else. It was an invitation inward.

And yet, there I was in Bali—a place where spirituality isn't scheduled but woven into the air. Here, shamans—Balian—are not fortune-tellers in the Western sense. They are healers, energy guides, keepers of balance between the seen and unseen worlds. People visit them not for predictions, but for alignment.

I told myself I'd go—partly out of curiosity, partly because this was a place where openness felt natural. Looking back, I see it wasn't really about doubting myself. It was about allowing the possibility that guidance could come from somewhere unexpected. And in leadership, that's not uncertainty. That's wisdom.

In a world driven by data and deadlines, my encounter with the shaman reminded me of the value of intuition, healing, and ancestral awareness. He didn't speak in corporate jargon, yet the message was unmistakable: To lead others, I must first confront the parts of me I had learned to silence. It wasn't mysticism. It was listening—with intention, without interruption, without fear.

That evening, I sat in stillness and let his words settle into places I hadn't touched in a long time. I meditated, not to seek answers, but to hear myself again—the parts of me that had been too tired, too loyal, or too afraid to speak.

By morning, something in me had softened. I woke with a quiet clarity, a sense that something had shifted, though I couldn't name it yet.

What he told me was something I already knew but had not yet said aloud: I had carried too much. Led too many. Stayed too long. Part of leadership, he reminded me, is knowing when to release the people, roles, and expectations that no longer align. That message landed hard. How much had I sacrificed in staying on, trying to protect and honor others? In doing so, I realized, I had betrayed something else entirely: myself.

Over breakfast, my friends offered reflections of who they saw in me—words I hadn't been ready to hear until now.

"The Awakening."

"The Phoenix."

"The Shrinking Violet, finally expanding."

I wept—not because I disagreed, but because I finally allowed myself to believe it. That I was not responsible for everyone's suffering. That pain—like labor—can precede something beautiful. That wholeness requires release.

That afternoon, I decided to honor that release in a different way.

And then there was the flower bath—a moment I didn't expect to matter as deeply as it did. I lowered myself into a pool overflowing with flower petals, and for the first time in a long time, I let beauty hold me—without guilt, without justification, without apology. It wasn't about luxury. It was about remembering softness.

After years of being the one who carried, who pushed, who solved, who led, I allowed myself to simply be adorned. In that warm water, surrounded by color and scent, I felt my body exhale in a way my mind had never permitted. The flower bath wasn't just aesthetic—it was the moment I surrendered to being cared for.

On my final day, just hours before our flight, I signed up for a mandala art class. No template. No prompt. Just colors, brushes, instinct. The instructor spoke little English, and for a moment, I wondered if I'd wasted my time. But then he handed me a blank sheet and gestured for me to begin.

I selected my palette, mixed the paints, and started to create. There was no deliverable, no performance. Just quiet creation—a visual record of the inner rearranging I had come to name. My artwork was interpreted, and here is what I got:

"This mandala reflects a journey inward—one that begins in calm contemplation and unfolds into radiant self-expression. The interplay of deep blues and fiery oranges mirrors the contrast between stillness and transformation, while the grounded greens and vibrant center express growth, resilience, and renewal. Through color and symmetry, I explored the balance of opposing forces and the beauty of blooming from within."

Bali didn't hand me a new identity. It reminded me of the one I had buried beneath deliverables and deadlines. The one who could trust before verifying. Who could lead without bracing. Who could breathe—before building.

And for the first time in a long time, I let that be enough.

From The Field To The Boardroom

Bali reminded me that renewal is not a side project—it's a leadership imperative. In organizations, we often push for transformation without making space for cleansing what no longer serves us. Just as the Melukat water purification ritual was about washing away what weighed me down, leaders must intentionally clear away outdated systems, toxic habits, and unspoken resentments before expecting their teams to thrive.

I learned that true change is not about adding more—more strategy, more policies, more action plans—but about creating space. In the same way that Balinese rituals honor the invisible energies shaping daily life, effective leadership acknowledges and tends to the unseen forces shaping team performance: trust, psychological safety, and a shared sense of purpose.

BALI:
LEADERSHIP LESSONS IN CLARITY

- Leadership is an inside-out practice. You can't sustainably lead others if you're out of alignment with yourself.

- Your nervous system is a leadership system. Urgency, bracing, and overfunctioning are not signs of strength—they're cues for recalibration.

- Trust doesn't require verification to be powerful. Extending trust empowers others to rise—and gives you permission to release.

- Culture doesn't need to be spoken to be felt. The most harmonious teams embody shared values naturally.

- Integration is more valuable than transformation. You don't need to become someone new—just more fully yourself.

- Sometimes leadership looks like letting go. Of roles, people, or old definitions of success—so something aligned can emerge.

PLACES THAT HELD ME IN BALI

Tirta Empul Temple—where water purification ceremony became release, and I felt layers of weight being washed away.

The Udaya Resort & Spa—where the flower bath turned rest into a ritual, and softness felt sacred again.

Mandala Art Studio—a space for creativity and presence, where expression replaced striving.

Lempuyang Temple at sunrise, where mist and light met in stillness, reminding me how quiet can be powerful.

Kecak Fire Dance at Uluwatu—rhythm and flame telling ancient stories of courage and community.

Goa Rajo Waterfall—a hidden sanctuary where nature insisted on surrender.

Dinner at the Cave (a subterranean restaurant) by Chef Ryan Clift, deep beneath the earth, where surprise and beauty met in darkness.

Chapter 2: Letting Go in Bali

○

BOWING TO STILLNESS IN JAPAN (THE ART OF INTENTIONAL LIVING)

> "In a land that reveres silence,
> I finally started to hear
> my own voice."

Tokyo runs like clockwork. Trains arrive within seconds of their scheduled time. Employees bow to show respect. While my initial thought was that the structure was constraint, I quickly came to realize that it was an enabler of high performance. Systems were created where expectations were crystal clear, allowing people to perform at their best. Rules were set so everyone started from the same baseline—freeing them to focus on anticipating the needs of those they served. In my case, the customer. Before I uttered a word, my problem was being addressed. My body language, simple gestures—these were noticed. My discomfort, my contentment—it was all seen. And people stood ready to ensure my comfort. It wasn't just directed toward me. It was how they treated one another. They moved in sync.

Japan moved with intention. There were rules—plenty of them—but they didn't feel restrictive. Instead, they felt like quiet invitations to be mindful, to honor the space and presence of others. The structure wasn't about control; it was about collective respect.

That word—respect—stayed with me. Respect is the foundation of trust, collaboration, and dignity. Respect is not weakness.

Interestingly, I had begun hearing the phrase "trust but verify" repeatedly on this leg of my journey, not from the Japanese, but from other travelers I encountered, many of them Western, just like those I encountered in Bali. A phrase that once lived in the background of how I was supposed to operate—especially in business. But here, in the hush of Japan's order, it struck a dissonant chord.

I've consciously worked to release that phrase. It goes against the grain of who I am and how I choose to lead. Why not just trust?

Trust, in its purest form, is empowering. It says to the person across from you, "I see you. I believe in you." It invites them to rise—to carry responsibility with pride, not fear.

Will mistakes happen? Of course. But so will growth. And the kind of growth that comes from being trusted is transformational. It fosters accountability, creativity, and loyalty—qualities no amount of verification can manufacture.

In Japan, I didn't just observe respect. I felt it—in every small gesture, every unspoken norm. It reminded me that leadership is not about control. It's about creating space for others to bring their best forward.

Every motion was intentional. The bow of a shopkeeper. The slow steeping of tea. The way an elderly man swept the temple steps—not to finish, but to be in the sweeping. Everything handed to you was offered with two hands and received the same way. There was no rush. No badge of honor for exhaustion.

Even during breakfast, I could feel the depth of observation—not staring for its own sake, but a kind of presence, a silent dance. They weren't just watching me; they were with me, attuned to every nuance. So much so that they knew what I needed before I did.

And yet, while they attuned to the energy around them, I realized how often I moved through my own world on autopilot, oblivious to my surroundings.

One morning, I answered a call—casual, nothing urgent— and spoke softly as I ate. But something felt off. It wasn't until I noticed the stillness around me that I realized: No one else was speaking. Not even in whispers. My voice, even muted, was an intrusion. It wasn't shame I felt—it was awakening. The understanding that silence, too, is sacred.

Another time, I was simply ... walking. Focused, brisk, lost in my own urgency. I didn't expect my energy to spill forward, but it did. The man ahead of me must've felt it—he paused, stepped aside, and let me pass. No words exchanged, just an instinctual dance of awareness. In that fleeting moment, I saw how movement, like sound, carries intention. Even strangers respond to what we bring into the world.

And then there was Shibuya Crossing—that surge of humanity I'd heard so much about. I stood at the edge and watched—hundreds, maybe more, moving across the intersection like a living organism. Everyone had somewhere to go, yet no one collided. It was chaos made elegant. When I finally stepped into it, I didn't feel lost. I felt part of something. A tide. A rhythm. A reminder that even in disorder, there is grace.

At first, Japan's order felt like the very thing I was trying to leave behind—the rules, the precision, the sense that every movement had a right and wrong. My journey was about loosening my grip, about letting the armor fall away. And yet here I was, in a place where even the trains seemed to bow to the clock, where sidewalks flowed like carefully choreographed dances, where tea was poured as if time itself depended on the angle of the wrist.

It took me days to see the difference. My own drive for perfection had always been tethered to fear—fear of being underestimated, dismissed, or torn down. Japan's intentionality was tethered to something else entirely: Care. Respect. The quiet dignity of doing even the smallest thing with purpose. The structure here didn't feel like a cage. It felt like a container—one that made room for stillness. And in that stillness, I began to wonder: Could discipline and freedom live in the same space? Could the very structure I had once run from actually create the conditions for my own voice to emerge?

That question lingered with me as I reflected on *ikigai*—the Japanese concept of "reason for being." It felt like the perfect intersection of what I had come here to understand: that purpose doesn't have to be born from pressure. It can come from alignment. From care. From showing up fully in whatever moment you're in—whether that's crossing a street with hundreds of strangers or quietly pouring a cup of tea.

It made me realize how far I'd traveled—not just in miles, but in mindset. For most of my life, success had been forged in fire, in reaction to bias, to opportunity, to being "the only one in the room." I had worn achievement like armor, believing grace was something you earned only after proving yourself. But here, grace seemed to come first. Success in Japan looked less like a battle won and more like a life well-lived.

And sometimes, that grace revealed itself in the smallest, most ordinary moments. My first quiet lesson came in the form of a Panasonic Caruru iron. It sat neatly on the hotel shelf, compact and unfamiliar. No English instructions. No helpful icons. Just elegant design, soft edges, and an assumption that I'd somehow know what to do. I didn't. So, I googled it. And in doing so, I found myself appreciating the thoughtfulness behind its form—every detail considered, nothing excessive, nothing random. Even an iron had dignity.

That moment—frustrating, amusing, and oddly grounding— reminded me of a much earlier chapter in my life. Many, many years ago, during my time as a process engineering intern at IBM, I was immersed in a culture obsessed with optimization. We were tasked with implementing the Japanese Kanban system—which, in the West, we often reduced to just-in-time inventory: minimize stock, eliminate waste, move faster, leaner, better. I remember being handed a thick manual filled with charts and process maps, as if the essence of Kanban could be distilled into a formula. We tried to make it work. But we couldn't—not fully. Over time, I began to understand why. Kanban wasn't just a process. It was a philosophy—a way of living rooted in awareness, respect, and an almost intuitive sense of timing and need. It wasn't about speed. It was about alignment.

Years later, walking through Tokyo's orderly streets and Kyoto's still gardens, it finally clicked. Kanban wasn't merely a system—it was a way of being. I saw it in the rhythm of the trains, the grace of the tea ceremony, the quiet between words. In Japan, there is reverence for the task at hand—whether it's folding laundry or serving a meal. There's an unspoken understanding that how you do something is just as important as what you're doing.

That same trust in rhythm and awareness showed up in unexpected places—like the Tokyo Street Kart Tours. Formerly known as Mario Kart, the experience allowed people to dress up in costumes and drive custom go-karts through the bustling streets of Tokyo, weaving past landmarks like Tokyo Tower and Shibuya Crossing, literally alongside cars and buses on major highways.

I chickened out and rode in the van that followed, but even from there, I felt the magic. No practice laps. No micromanaging. No excessive instructions.

Just: Get in and drive.

At one point, the karts stopped on a bridge for a break. I looked out at the organized chaos around me and thought: *There's no way this could work back home—too much risk, too little trust.* But here, it worked flawlessly. Everyone moved to the same unspoken beat. A rhythm that, once you felt it, made everything possible.

Even the meals in Japan mirrored this culture of intention. Portions were modest—not because of scarcity, but because nothing was wasted. Every dish was thoughtful, balanced, and beautifully presented. And it was considered disrespectful not to finish what was offered.

At first, I was struck by how small the servings were. But over time, I realized nothing more was needed. It wasn't just the food that reflected restraint—it was the *pace.* Meals were eaten slowly, each bite carefully chewed, giving the body time to digest and the mind time to catch up—to recognize fullness and satisfaction.

There was dignity in that rhythm. A quiet trust that enough is truly enough.

It was, in many ways, a training of the mind—not to crave more, but to be present with what is. It made me wonder how often, in life and in leadership, we overfill—our plates, our schedules, our conversations—out of habit, not necessity.

Here, even nourishment was a practice in presence.

It was somewhere between Tokyo and Kyoto, riding the Shinkansen as the countryside blurred past, that ikigai came across my mind again.

Back home, I was used to using the Venn diagram as a career tool—a tidy framework of quadrants and logic. But on that train, with rice fields flashing like brushstrokes and mist-covered hills rising in soft silence, ikigai felt like something older. Wiser. Less about optimization, more about alignment.

The landscape—small towns, shrines, winding rivers—moved too quickly to grasp, yet somehow the motion felt steady, unhurried. It mirrored the questions beginning to surface in me:

- What do you love?
- What are you good at?
- What does the world need?
- What can you be paid for?

Each question landed deeper than before, less intellectual, more embodied. By the time the train began to slow, I came to the realization that ikigai wasn't something you *diagram*—it was something you *feel your way into.*

Kyoto greeted me with the hush of falling leaves—golden ginkgo drifting through temple gardens like time itself had slowed to a deliberate whisper.

I checked into Nazuna Kyoto Gosho, a traditional ryokan, where I was asked to remove my shoes and leave them at the entrance. It was a small gesture, yet it felt symbolic—a quiet invitation to step into another way of being. Nothing felt rushed here. Meals arrived like poetry: seasonal, delicate, intentional. The room held no clutter, only space. And somehow, that space held me.

I walked through the stone pathways of Nanzen-ji with the reverence of someone entering both a sacred space and a confrontation. The world outside had always moved fast. I had matched its speed. Outrun its expectations. Outsmarted its assumptions.

But here ... nothing chased me.

The silence didn't feel empty; it felt architectural. Designed. Deliberate. A reminder that stillness is not stagnation—it is strategy.

The next morning, I set out for the Arashiyama Bamboo Forest. The air was cool, the kind that wakes every sense without jarring them. The path—*Chikurin-no-Komichi*—curved gently through towering stalks of mōsō bamboo that swayed almost imperceptibly, their hollow trunks whispering in the wind.

The sound wasn't quite a rustle—more like a conversation between air and wood, ancient and alive.

I learned that the grove has stood since the Heian period, when Kyoto was the imperial capital and nobles planted bamboo as living sanctuaries—places to quiet the mind and soften ambition. Even now, light filtered through the green columns like prayer.

In Japanese culture, bamboo embodies resilience and grace: It bends but does not break. Moves swiftly, yet always upward. Thrives in clusters, never alone.

As I walked, I thought of leadership the same way—rooted, flexible, collective.

Each step echoed softly, then disappeared into stillness. The forest seemed to insist on presence.

By the time I returned to the city, the rhythm of that grove stayed with me. Kyoto moved differently—slower, deeper, deliberately.

For years, I had operated squarely in two quadrants: What I was good at. What I could be paid for. Finance. Strategy. Compliance. I knew how to run lean, how to hit targets, how to deliver results under pressure.

But what I loved? What the world needed—from *me*?

I hadn't asked those questions in a long time. Maybe ever.

It reminded me of my conversation with the shaman in Bali—how he had urged me to release what no longer served me so I could step into alignment. Sitting in that uncluttered ryokan room, I realized that alignment isn't always a single, dramatic moment; sometimes it's a quiet accumulation of choices that make space for what matters. The shaman's words had been the catalyst, but Kyoto gave me the conditions to hear them differently—to see that my ikigai wasn't something to chase, but something to uncover by stripping away the noise.

There was a time when success was my survival strategy. When proving I belonged in rooms no one expected me to enter became the mission. I had mastered performance. But purpose? Purpose had become buried under deliverables, slide decks, and the pursuit of legitimacy.

And yet, here—surrounded by a culture that revered simplicity, intentionality, and grace—I began to wonder if I could lead differently. Live differently. If I could reenter my own story not just as an executor, but as an author.

Maybe ikigai wasn't something you chased. Maybe it was something you returned to.

In the stillness, I didn't feel empty. I felt restored. I allowed myself to be soft. Unseen. Unproducing.

And in that stillness, I met the version of me that was tired of performing. She didn't need applause. She needed peace. Don't we all? Japan didn't offer me clarity in restraint. It reminded me that leadership isn't about control—it's about design. It's about allowing space, trusting rhythm, and honoring each step of the process with care. The same way that the Caruru iron was crafted. The same way that the garden was raked. The same way, I realized, I wanted to begin crafting the next chapter of my life.

With less noise. More intention. And room for something sacred to take root.

In Japan, stillness taught me something profound: We live inside the worlds we believe in. What we perceive—whether grounded in truth or stitched together from fragments—becomes our reality. The mind can summon a future or a fear, and once it does, we begin to live as if it were already true.

I saw this play out on an ordinary afternoon. My tour had been curated just for me, each stop carefully chosen. At one point, I mentioned casually to my tour guide that someone I knew who was visiting Japan at the same time might pass by to say hello. In that instant, something shifted in the guide. His expression changed—almost imperceptibly, but enough to feel. He wasn't Japanese, and perhaps that mattered; maybe it was a cultural lens, or maybe it was something else entirely. I could almost see the story forming behind his eyes—a quiet suspicion that she was following us, shadowing the tour. In his mind, the script had already been written. From that moment on, his responses weren't to what was unfolding, but to what he had decided was unfolding.

I found myself both entertained and fascinated by it—watching, almost as a study, how quickly perception can eclipse truth and how easily a single assumption can rewrite an entire story.

And it reminded me: Perception is never neutral. It's filtered through the cultures we're born into, the histories we carry, and the stories we tell ourselves. People rarely respond to what *is*; they respond to the picture they've already painted in their minds.

That understanding followed me back to a memory from home. During a move, a small box of old coins went missing. Almost immediately, the assumption was made that the coins had been stolen. There was no pause, no inquiry—only certainty. The conclusion fit an existing narrative, so it became fact.

What went unnoticed was another explanation. The coins had been placed into pockets for safekeeping, tucked away to prevent them from scattering or being lost in the chaos. An act of care had been misread as an act of harm.

Nothing about the situation itself had changed. Only the lens.

I had the opportunity to go to the Seiunji Temple—one of the temples along the Yanaka Seven Lucky Gods pilgrimage route. The pilgrimage itself is a centuries-old tradition, inviting worshippers to walk slowly through each temple and reflect on blessings, perspective, and purpose.

I learned that Seiunji offers omikuji, the traditional fortune slips tied to Japanese ideas of luck, fate, and the unseen. The slips are categorized from *dai-kichi* (great blessing) to *dai-kyo* (very bad luck). It isn't a game of prediction—it's a ritual of surrender, an intentional pause to let the divine (or the random) speak.

Before drawing an omikuji, there's a small purification rite. I rinsed my left hand, then my right, and lightly rinsed my mouth at the temizuya—symbolically entering the sacred space with a clear mind and open heart. I placed a small coin in the offering box near the omikuji stand as a gesture of respect, then received a little key and opened one of the wooden drawers. Inside was a folded slip with neatly printed characters and a cryptic message—as if the universe had a slightly mischievous sense of humor.

Standing there with the paper in my hand, I paused.

Do I believe in luck? Absolutely not. But I do believe that answers are often right in front of us, waiting for that one moment when we're finally willing to see them.

As a leader, I've learned that direction is rarely hidden. It's simply obscured—by noise, urgency, ego, and fear. The fortune slip wasn't magic—it was a mirror. Its value wasn't in predicting what would happen next. Its value was in my willingness to look honestly and hear what I already knew.

My slip revealed dai-kichi—best fortune—the highest level, the one that signals that the path ahead, if walked with integrity and courage, will lead exactly where it's meant to. I didn't read it as *prediction*. I read it as permission—permission to trust the direction I was already headed.

I've always believed that each of us has a purpose, and that the closer we move toward our ikigai—our true reason for being—the more clearly the universe reflects it back to us. This fortune didn't tell me something new. It affirmed what I had been sensing for a long time: *I am in control of where I go and how I choose to lead.*

Common levels of omikuji from high to low:
- Dai-kichi (best fortune)—the highest blessing
- Kichi (good fortune)—favorable circumstances
- Chu-kichi (moderate fortune)—generally positive with minor challenges
- Sho-kichi (small fortune)—modest blessing or guidance
- Sue-kichi (future fortune)—good fortune emerging later
- Kyo (bad fortune)—a warning or unfavorable situation
- Dai-kyo (very bad fortune)—significant obstacles or difficult times

My slip spoke of plans prospering, journeys flowing smoothly, and relationships deepening. I didn't take that as fate. I took it as alignment—as a reminder that when preparation meets timing, and when intentional choices align with inner truth, the path begins to open.

Japan didn't offer me clarity through restraint alone—it reminded me that leadership isn't about control; it's about design. It's about allowing space, trusting rhythm, and honoring each step of the process with care. The same way the Caruru iron was crafted. The same way the garden was raked. The same way, I realized, I want to begin crafting the next chapter of my life: With less noise. More intention. And room for something sacred to take root.

FROM THE FIELD TO THE BOARDROOM

In Japan, I saw how discipline and grace can coexist—how intentional structure doesn't confine people, but enables them to excel. The clarity of systems, the respect embedded in daily interactions, and the care in even the smallest actions reminded me that high performance isn't built on pressure alone. In organizations, just like in Tokyo's trains or Kyoto's tea ceremonies, structure can be the very thing that creates the freedom to innovate.

The lesson? When you design systems that are clear, respectful, and purposeful, you give your teams the space to show up fully—and the confidence to move in harmony without constant supervision.

JAPAN:
LEADERSHIP LESSONS IN STILLNESS AND PRECISION

- Stillness is not stagnation. In a world obsessed with urgency, Japan reminded me that silence, pause, and observation can be powerful strategic tools. Leadership doesn't always have to be loud to be effective. The stillness is the strategy.

- Lead with intention, not impulse. Whether it was the tea ceremony, the care in packaging, or the timing of a bow—everything had purpose. It taught me that excellence comes not just from effort, but from thoughtful design and deliberate execution.

- Boundaries are a form of respect. The culture's emphasis on space, order, and rhythm offered a powerful counterpoint to overexertion. It reminded me that protecting your energy—and honoring that of others—is foundational to sustainable leadership.

- Elegance in leadership isn't about excess. It's about refinement. Simplicity. The ability to remove the unnecessary so that what matters most can shine through—whether in a decision, a team dynamic, or a strategy.

- Harmony matters. Japan taught me that leadership isn't just about driving forward—it's also about aligning. With people. With place. With timing. Harmony fosters resilience and collective momentum.

Places That Held Me in Japan

Shibuya Crossing: A living metaphor of movement and harmony.

Tokyo Station Hotel: A place that felt like grandeur wrapped in restraint; an architectural masterpiece where history and modernity meet beneath arched ceilings and soft light.

Shinkansen Bullet Train: It felt like meditation in motion, teaching me that speed doesn't have to mean urgency.

Kyoto's temples, gardens, and autumn stillness: Considered the soul of Japan, where intention lived in every detail.

Arashiyama Bamboo Forest: Where I came to understand that alignment is what steadies us, even when the world moves.

Chapter 3: Bowing to Stillness in Japan

CHAPTER 4

REMEMBERING IN SOUTH KOREA

> " What do you keep chasing,
> even when no one's watching? "

When I first landed in South Korea, I wondered if I had miscalculated—taken a step backward on my healing journey. Our driver barely spoke. There was no warm welcome, no small talk—just pure efficiency. It felt cold compared to the spirit of Bali or the silence of Japan, which had both met me with a kind of gentle reverence. By contrast, Seoul was in motion before I had even caught my breath.

But maybe that was the point.

By the time I arrived, the noise of the company I had left behind had finally begun to fade. I had soaked in the ritual of Bali. I had bowed into the stillness of Japan. The grip of performance was beginning to loosen. But the ache to achieve—the urge to prove, to plan, to optimize—still hummed beneath my skin. South Korea brought it to the surface.

I stayed in Hongdae, one of Seoul's most vibrant, youthful, and unapologetically creative neighborhoods. It radiated a raw, magnetic energy that pulsed through the streets—bold, unfiltered, alive. I didn't feel out of place. I felt invisible in the best way.

At check-in, a sign stood at the center of the registration desk, impossible to miss: Respect Employees. Hongdae delivered its message clearly, without room for misunderstanding.

Seoul is built on discipline. Trains run with precision. Cafés buzz well past midnight, filled with students buried in study. Even beauty here feels deliberate—sculpted, refined, perfected. Clinics and cosmetic shops line the streets like a second skyline. There is order in every detail: clean lines, quiet hierarchy, measured ambition. Striking, and for someone like me, deeply familiar.

The city's rhythm stirred something old in me—the part taught that excellence was survival, that worth was earned through output, that rest must be justified. Even the room key carried its own charge: To power the lights, you had to insert a card that read *"Have a Powerful Day."* A small thing, but it jolted me—a reminder that power for the sake of power is just that: power. Empty.

Soon, I found myself making lists again. Pages of business ideas, advisory concepts, next steps. I told myself I was brainstorming, keeping my mind sharp. But I knew better. Even in stillness, I was reaching for momentum.

I had left the job. I had stepped away from the culture. But the wiring—the pattern—was still very much alive.

It wasn't until I visited Jogyesa Temple, hidden quietly among glass towers and luxury storefronts, that I finally exhaled. This temple is the spiritual heart of Korean Zen Buddhism. A monk walked past me slowly, the steady beat of a drum marking the beginning of a service. I listened as the monks in gray robes chanted sutras and bowed in meditative rhythms. Lanterns swayed in the autumn breeze. No one asked anything of me there. The world simply let me sit and allowed me to peek into centuries-old tradition.

And in that stillness, the truth arrived—gently, but unmistakably:

I am not my performance. I never was.

The business wins, the contracts, the growth I led—they were real. But they weren't *me*. They were things I created. Evidence of my capability, yes. But not proof of my essence.

After a few days in Seoul, the rhythm of the city began to feel almost intimate—structured yet intense, youthful yet burdened. There was a beautiful urgency in the rain-soaked lines of students waiting outside a K-pop pop-up store, their perfectly styled looks dissolving in the downpour.

But I needed to breathe.

I took a day trip to Gangwon Province, chasing silence and altitude. The two-hour drive from Hongdae to Alpaca World wound through lush, layered mountains—the green backbone of a country where nearly seventy percent of the land rises and folds into itself. The journey felt meditative, a slow untangling from the intensity of the city. As the mountains rolled past, I thought about pace, about expansion, about what grows when we let the land—or ourselves—rest.

Among alpacas and open fields, something soft and joyful stirred in me. I fed them, their gentle faces pressing toward my hands, and for the first time in days, I laughed—an unguarded, belly-deep sound. Later, I rode rail bikes through forested hillsides, wind in my face, laughter trailing behind me like a tailwind. The rail bikes—open-air pedal cars that followed old train tracks through quiet tunnels and thick patches of forest—moved with a rhythm that was unforced. Pedal by pedal, we advanced, not quickly but steadily, with only the sound of the track beneath us and the occasional breeze brushing our cheeks.

It wasn't about speed or arrival. It was motion for the sake of experience—a rare kind of movement that asked nothing from me but presence. I was simply there, breathing, feeling the gentle resistance between ambition and stillness—the same tension I'd noticed throughout my time in South Korea. A country racing forward in innovation, yet still rooted in ceremony and quiet tradition. A place where skyscrapers rise beside temples, and fast trains pause at villages untouched by time.

Somewhere on that winding drive toward Alpaca World, our driver mentioned, almost casually, that North Korea was only fifty or sixty miles away. In the same breath, he talked about how PSY's "Gangnam Style" once broke the internet and made the world suddenly curious about this little peninsula—the same Korea we were driving through, not watching on a screen. And it struck me: What separates the two Koreas isn't an ocean or a mountain range, but a 2.5-mile-wide strip of land called the DMZ—a quiet green belt threaded with land mines, fences, guard posts, and the unresolved tension of a war that never officially ended. It was surreal to be headed to feed alpacas in peaceful mountain air while knowing that, just beyond the next bend, peace and fragility pressed right against each other.

In many ways, it mirrored where I stood as a leader—constantly accelerating, constantly proving, and yet longing for a more intentional rhythm. The rail bike didn't demand effort; it invited alignment. It reminded me that not all forward motion requires push. Sometimes, movement is most powerful when it's done with ease.

After the ride, I took a short ferry to Nami Island. Named for a Joseon-era general, the island unfolded in tree-lined paths that whispered of the past. It felt suspended in time—not quite old, not quite new. Like me, it was in transition.

Before leaving, I wandered into a quiet corner of the island and stopped at the Wall of Names—an installation honoring longtime employees. In a world that too often treats workers as invisible labor behind seamless experiences, Nami chose to showcase them: gardeners, cooks, ferry operators, artists. Each name told a quiet story of contribution, of legacy, of being seen.

I stood there longer than I expected, reading names I didn't know. But I didn't need to know them. I could feel them—the humility, the pride, the reminder that the magic of a place isn't just in its trees or trails, but in the people who make it whole.

As a leader, I've delivered more presentations than I can count—about strategy, metrics, impact. But that wall told me something else: *Remember the hands that hold it all together.* Honor the unseen. Build spaces where people know they matter, even when they're not in the room.

Leaving Nami Island, I noticed how the Han River divides the city of Seoul—and, symbolically, the country. To the south, Gangnam pulses with ambition and affluence, made famous by a viral song but rooted in real power. To the north, Gangbuk holds the old soul of the city—palaces, temples, Hanok villages that have endured for centuries. It was like walking through two Koreas: one future-facing, one memory-keeping.

Back in Seoul, beneath the neon and noise, I sensed something else—a quiet, collective unease. Korea, like many nations, is facing a demographic cliff: a declining birth rate, an aging population. On paper, it's an economic problem; on the streets, it feels like a cultural reckoning. Seoul is electric with youth—K-pop, fashion, themed cafés—yet beneath the surface, a deeper question hums: *Who will carry the country forward, and at what cost?*

Maybe that's the deeper lesson I carried home—that both nations and leaders must learn how to grow without losing their soul. That progress without pause is unsustainable. And that stillness, too, is a form of strength.

It reminded me of the questions I had begun to ask myself: What gets passed down? What's preserved? What fades? What kind of world—or company, or legacy—have I helped steward? And was it built with endurance in mind?

These weren't abstract thoughts. I've helped build organizations. Scaled them. Led people. But growth that doesn't account for sustainability—human sustainability—eventually collapses. Korea's quiet demographic tension reflected my own inner questions about leadership, transition, and what it means to truly create something enduring.

And I realized: Korea, like me, is holding its breath—suspended between what was and what's next, seeking harmony while negotiating ambition.

That, too, is my story.

As we returned from the mountains, the city skyline reappearing on the horizon, I couldn't help but think of the parallels between this land and the organizations I've led. Growth is often mistaken for movement, but real sustainability—in a country or a company—depends on balance. Korea's quiet tension between legacy and innovation reminded me that effective leadership isn't just about driving forward. It's about knowing when to pause. When to listen. When to recalibrate.

Around this time, I learned that a pastor from back home—a longtime family friend and, at times, my spiritual anchor—happened to be in South Korea too. We hadn't planned it; it was simply a convergence. I reached out to see if we could meet, but our schedules didn't align. Still, we spoke—a brief conversation that carried the warmth of familiarity across time and distance.

His presence, even from a distance, reminded me that I wasn't drifting. I was aligning. That even thousands of miles from home, my compass—my values, my calling, my sense of what matters—remained intact.

Finding your True North isn't just about stillness or solitude. Sometimes, it's confirmed in the quiet ways your world reflects back to you that you're on the right path. That the work of undoing and becoming is, in itself, progress.

And in that awareness, I found clarity: The best leaders don't just manage change—they navigate contradiction with grace.

In Korea, I didn't shed another layer.

I simply saw it more clearly.

I had been clinging to achievement as identity—mistaking output for worth, motion for meaning. But safety built on exhaustion is not safety at all.

So, I put the pen down. I let the lists go.

I walked the streets of Seoul without needing them to mean anything.

I allowed myself to just be—not strategic, not successful, not productive.

Just whole.

And soon, I would carry that wholeness with me across continents—to Tanzania and Zanzibar.

Not to escape, but to deepen. To listen to a different rhythm. To explore a new kind of leadership rooted not just in strategy, but in connection, land, and legacy.

Because this journey isn't just about leaving something behind. It's about returning to something deeper.

From The Field To The Boardroom

South Korea showed me the power of discipline paired with quiet pride. The country runs on precision—trains arriving within seconds, cafés buzzing late into the night with students deep in study, and a social order that creates a sense of shared responsibility. Even in Hongdae's raw, creative energy, there was an underlying structure that allowed self-expression to flourish.

In leadership, the same balance is critical: Structure should enable freedom, not stifle it. Systems and processes exist not to control every move, but to create a foundation that frees people to perform at their best. The best leaders know when to enforce the standard and when to step aside so talent can take the lead.

And just like the "Respect Employees" sign I saw at hotel check-in, workplace culture isn't an afterthought. It's embedded in how people interact, how workspaces are designed, and how success is measured. South Korea reminded me that respect isn't a slogan; it's a practice—and when it's consistently upheld, it becomes a competitive advantage.

SOUTH KOREA:
LEADERSHIP LESSONS IN HARMONY AND DUALITY

- Integration over opposition: Modernity and tradition are not adversaries—they coexist. Neon skylines rise beside ancient temples, and both command reverence. Leadership too can hold dualities: strength and softness, logic and intuition, drive and rest. How you integrate them is the true mastery.

- Collective strength over individual control: Korea challenged my Enneagram 8 instinct to go at it alone. Harmony doesn't mean conformity; it means coordination. I witnessed shared purpose thriving not through dominance but through deep listening and mutual flow.

- Respect as a form of power: Respect is not submission—it's acknowledgment. Deference, when rooted in awareness rather than hierarchy, can be one of the quietest yet most transformative forms of influence.

Places That Held Me in South Korea

Gangwon Province – a landscape that felt wide open and available. I learned that space is not empty; it is restorative. In that quiet expanse, my thoughts unraveled without resistance.

Alpaca World – watching alpacas approach with innocent curiosity, unconcerned with status or productivity. I was simply human, laughing at their soft noses and awkward stature.

Bongeunsa Temple – another dimension, with skyscrapers hovering beyond the wall, reminding me that achievement and stillness can coexist.

Nami Island – a gentle escape where I wandered aimlessly and embraced the life I've been given.

Seoul – impossible not to feel its momentum. It showed me striving is powerful when we understand what we're striving for.

Jogyesa Temple – devotion felt intimate, lanterns floating overhead like visible prayers, each carrying a wish, hope, or memory.

ALPACAWorld

LEGACY IN TANZANIA/ZANZIBAR

" *Sometimes the land doesn't give you answers—it gives you back to yourself.* "

On the flight to Tanzania, I watched the film *Chevalier*, the story of Joseph Bologne—an accomplished violinist, composer, and fencer, and the son of an enslaved African woman and a French plantation owner. He lived in an era that constantly tried to limit him because of his mixed ancestry despite his accomplishments. In one scene, Bologne recalls his father's advice: Life will confront you with injustice and cruelty, so you must always be excellent. Never give anyone a reason to tear you down.

That line landed like a stone in my chest. Because I had lived it. Excellence as armor. Achievement as a shield. My whole life, I had operated from that place—believing that if I just performed at a higher level, delivered more, proved my worth over and over, I could outrun bias, criticism, or exclusion.

But as I watched, I began to wonder—what had this cost him? The constant vigilance. The exhaustion of working toward flawlessness just to hold your place. The quiet ache of knowing your acceptance was always conditional, granted not for who you were but for what you produced. I thought about my own career, about the boardrooms and conference calls where I wasn't sure if people saw me or only the results I delivered.

In that moment, I realized: The armor that keeps you safe also keeps you separate. The walls that protect you are the same ones that can confine you.

That was the quiet hinge I didn't see coming—a subtle shift from defending my place to questioning why I felt I had to defend it at all.

As the film ended, another truth surfaced—one that lingered longer than the music. For all of Joseph Bologne's brilliance, history still found a way to forget him. His excellence earned him entry into rooms that were never meant to hold him, but it did not secure his permanence. When the performance stopped, there was almost nothing left to show for the lifetime spent proving himself worthy to remain.

That realization unsettled me. Not because he failed—but because he succeeded and it still wasn't enough. Excellence, I saw, can buy proximity, but not preservation. And I couldn't help but wonder how many of us—myself included—spend our lives perfecting armor for systems that were never designed to remember us once we stop performing.

We arrived. We began our time in Tanzania at a peaceful lodge in Arusha, nestled in the shadow of Mount Kilimanjaro. Even when hidden behind clouds, the mountain carried an unmistakable weight. Mount Kilimanjaro wasn't loud or demanding, yet its presence shaped everything around it. It stood as a kind of guardian—reminding me of endurance, ascent, and the quiet strength of things that do not need to prove themselves to be undeniable. Arusha felt like a gentle entry point into East Africa—a place where time slowed and conversations lingered.

Our visit to the Cultural Heritage Centre was more than just a stop on the itinerary. It was an immersive walk through Tanzania's art, history, and soul—a powerful reminder of the importance of storytelling and heritage in shaping identity. Even in the structure and layout of the center, there was a sense of reverence, rootedness, and quiet dignity. We were greeted with drummers that signaled a welcoming, a feeling of belonging. It made me feel like I was home.

The next morning, as we made our way to Swala Camp, I hadn't realized the journey itself would be a game drive. I was unprepared for what was about to unfold. Fear rose fast—instinctive and uninvited—catching me off guard. Memories surfaced without warning: walking into a robbery and finding a gun pointed at my head, being chased and bitten by a dog, coming home to find my apartment broken into. But beneath those moments lived something older—a vigilance shaped long before adulthood.

I wasn't a quiet child; I spoke up, pushed back, questioned what didn't feel right. But in the environment I grew up in, that defiance sometimes brought consequences I hadn't intended—consequences that fell on others. Over time, I learned a painful lesson: My voice had power, but it could also bring harm. So, I began to shrink in other ways—not being silent, but careful. Not invisible, but watchful. I smiled to ease tension, softened edges to keep peace, and carried the guilt of believing that my strength had a cost.

Even as an adult—confident, capable, leading teams and organizations—my nervous system never forgot that early equation: that safety required constant scanning, calculating, adjusting. That being fully myself might come at someone else's expense.

That same tension found me again in the jeep. My body remembered before my mind did. The open air, the stillness, the lions lounging in the grass—it all stirred the same primal sense of exposure I'd spent a lifetime managing. My heart raced; my chest tightened. I tried to steady my breath, to hold myself together, but tears came anyway—quiet, involuntary, cleansing.

Our driver, calm but watchful, sensed my fear. His voice, steady and assured, broke through the silence: *You're okay. You're safe.* Such simple words, yet they landed somewhere deep—a reminder that safety didn't have to come from control or concealment. In that moment, my well-rehearsed composure gave way to something more honest: surrender.

When we transitioned to Sanctuary Swala Camp in Tarangire National Park, the tone deepened. Our accommodations were uniquely tethered to a towering baobab tree—a symbol of resilience and rootedness. Our tent was connected to that very tree. Two years earlier, my best friend had spoken about her deep connection to the baobab tree—how she drew strength and rootedness from its presence. And now, here I was, tethered to the same tree she had once described, as if the land itself was stitching together our stories. What she found in it, I could now feel: resilience, continuity, and belonging.

Life at the camp carried its own quiet intensity. I wasn't permitted to walk alone to my tent after dark or to dinner—the wilderness was too alive, too close. A walkie-talkie sat on the nightstand by my bed, my only line of contact in case of an emergency. Lying awake at night, the canvas walls felt impossibly thin against whatever might be moving outside. Fear would flicker—what was lurking just beyond reach?—but it was also part of the truth of being there: To live alongside the wild is to surrender the illusion of control. Even dinner, served outside beneath the stars, carried that edge of wonder and unease. As we ate, elephants moved in the distance, their massive silhouettes shifting in and out of the dark—unbothered, commanding, and free.

At night, the sounds of the wild pressed closer: rustling trees, distant calls, the primal rhythm of life continuing just beyond reach. Each day, I came face-to-face with the fears I had long hidden from. One particular evening we were on our way back to the campsite when my travel partner, holding her phone up to capture the fading light, suddenly gasped—it had slipped from her hands and tumbled out of the open-air jeep. The driver stopped instantly, his instincts sharp. Without hesitation, he decided we'd go back to find it.

I couldn't believe it. My heart sank. It was getting dark, and I knew what that meant—soon the nocturnal animals would come alive. Every story I'd heard about what happened after dusk in the bush ran through my mind. I wanted to keep going, to reach the safety of the camp. But the driver was calm, confident, and certain.

He estimated that we had driven no more than a mile since it fell, so he began to backtrack slowly. When we reached the area where he thought it might have dropped, he stopped the jeep, and we began scanning the field—searching with our eyes, straining to see anything that might glint or glimmer in the tall grass. The air was heavy, charged with tension. I was angry—angry that we were retracing our path, angry that my travel partner's mistake now felt like a collective risk. The stillness of the evening had shifted; the air felt different now. Every sound—the rustle in the brush, the distant cry of something unseen—set my nerves on edge.

Fear and frustration tangled inside me. I cried quietly, the kind of tears that come when you realize how little control you truly have. I thought, *this could be it*—that this might be how my story ended: swallowed by darkness, undone by a moment that wasn't even mine.

We searched for what felt like forever, the driver's eyes sweeping back and forth across the field, headlights cutting through the tall grass, our hearts pounding in sync with the silence. And then, just as he started to shift the jeep forward again, a voice broke through the dark: *"There it is."*

The phone—nestled in between the grass and the dirt, glinting faintly in the beam of the headlights.

Relief flooded me so quickly it made me dizzy. It wasn't just about the phone. It was about what the moment revealed—how easily fear can hijack reason, how quickly control can crumble when the illusion of safety falls away.

After the ride, I realized the fear wasn't just about lions or the wilderness. It was about exposure—about being seen in a moment I couldn't manage or predict. For so long, invisibility had kept me safe. But it had also kept me small. That day, somewhere between fear and release, I understood that hiding—even under the guise of strength—was no longer serving me. The same instinct that once protected me was now keeping me from embracing life fully.

And then, as if Tanzania herself had been waiting for me to exhale, the fear softened. What replaced it wasn't relief—it was awe. Out on the open plains of the Serengeti, I felt small, but in the best possible way. The horizon stretched farther than my eyes could reach, and everywhere I looked, life pulsed with motion. Herds of wildebeest and zebras moved together, their hooves stirring dust that shimmered in the sun. Elephants passed slowly, deliberate and unbothered, their calm presence a kind of authority that needed no noise. Baboons darted through the brush—chaotic, playful, purposeful.

I hadn't arrived during the famed Great Migration, but it hardly mattered. The land was alive. To sit in that vastness, to witness nature's unforced rhythm, was humbling. It reminded me that survival depends on movement—whether for the wildebeest on the plains or for me, navigating reinvention at sixty. Sometimes that means staying with the herd; other times, it means daring to step away.

The silence between sightings was just as powerful as the moments when the land erupted in motion. There was no need for words—only the wind through the grasses, the rumble of distant thunder, the low call of an elephant somewhere unseen. It felt as if Tanzania was whispering: *You are part of something larger—more enduring, more connected than you realize.*

Tanzania wasn't just offering me rest. It was offering me permission to be seen—and to be still.

I arrived with the weight of past chapters still gently echoing in my body. Bali had helped me soften. Japan reminded me of structure and grace. South Korea stirred old patterns I thought I had shed. Each stop had stripped something away. But it was here that I felt roots begin to form.

The landscape moved slowly, intentionally. Herds migrated with rhythm, not rush. Predators waited, not pounced. The entire ecosystem was calibrated to balance, not domination. It reminded me of what leadership could be: balance, awareness, timing.

No one in the wild apologizes for resting. They do it because it sustains life.

Later, on a game drive, I encountered a family of elephants—majestic, unbothered, entirely in command of their space. I saw lions resting in the shade, unhurried and powerful. These animals did not operate from fear. They moved with knowing. With presence. They didn't shrink. They didn't strive. They simply were.

But Tanzania is not one story—it is many. We ended our journey in Zanzibar, and almost immediately, I felt a shift in the energy. It was heavier, less content. The pride and dignity I'd witnessed among Tanzanians on the mainland seemed absent here. Many employees appeared discontent, their expressions and body language lacking the ease I had seen earlier in the trip.

Later, I learned about Zanzibar's complex history—the 1963 political upheaval when Zanzibar gained its independence and merged with Tanganyika to form modern-day Tanzania. This merger reminded me of a corporate merger and acquisition: two distinct cultures, systems, and rhythms trying to become one. But in Zanzibar, it felt as though the integration hadn't fully landed. One system had yet to emerge as the guiding force for the whole.

In a quiet conversation with a local community leader, something clicked. He described leadership as a responsibility of both ancestors and descendants. "You don't lead for yourself," he said. "You lead so the village will still be here when you are gone."

That insight stayed with me.

Because what if we led companies that way? Not driven by fear or ego, but with a deep commitment to legacy. What if growth meant more than just scale—what if it meant building something sustainable and worthy of inheritance?

The truth is, our systems back home are not built for that. They reward immediacy—quarterly wins, fast results, rapid expansion. Leaders are pressured to deliver now, even if it costs the future. But legacy requires a different kind of courage: the willingness to think beyond the next metric, the next meeting, the next moment. It asks us to plant seeds we may never personally see bloom.

That night, I wrote a note to myself: Lead like the land. Steady. Observant. Grounded. Unapologetically enough.

Every meaningful journey has its unplanned moments. For me, they came in quick succession—a sea urchin sting that sent one of my travel partners rushing to the doctor's office, a startled sea turtle that bit another's leg mid-feed (hello, tetanus shot), and a heart-stopping moment when one of our vans clipped a motorcyclist on the way to the airport (the injuries were serious). These weren't the memories I planned to bring home, but they became their own strange punctuation marks in an otherwise spiritual journey—reminders that even in stillness, life has a way of asserting itself.

Another unplanned moment was a ride on a dhow—a handcrafted wooden sailing vessel woven into centuries of maritime history. These boats once carried goods, traders, families, and entire migrations between East Africa, Arabia, and the Indian Subcontinent. As we sailed, I felt as if time blurred. The men on board played drums that grew louder, faster, more insistent, pulling something ancient to the surface. It awakened a bittersweet undertow of memory—of freedom and forced passage, of movement chosen and movement coerced. It was heavy, the kind of heaviness that doesn't weigh you down but opens something inside you.

That feeling would deepen later that evening when I stepped out for dinner and encountered a performance by the Freedom Dancers. Drums rose into the night, vibrant and alive, as the dancers moved as if they were pulling history through their bodies. Each beat was more than performance—it was testimony. Their movements carried the memory of captivity and the unbreakable will to be free. But woven into that history was something else too—joy, resilience, and reclamation. Their dance was an act of remembering and an act of release.

Watching them, I realized they were not only honoring the past but also embodying liberation in the present. The Serengeti had shown me what survival looked like in its purest form— the endless rhythm of life pressing forward. But the dancers in Zanzibar reminded me that survival alone is not enough. To survive is to endure; to dance is to reclaim freedom, to live fully, to move beyond endurance into expression.

The cadence of their bodies seemed to echo my own journey. I was no longer carrying armor. I was learning to move differently, to claim a rhythm that was mine, not bound by fear or striving.

As I prepared to leave, I wasn't planning the next big thing. I wasn't engineering a rebrand or sketching out a business plan. I was tending to the inner architecture of what kind of leader I wanted to be moving forward.

Because the next chapter won't be built by striving. It will be built by returning.

Returning to purpose. To rhythm. To what truly sustains. And Tanzania reminded me: Legacy isn't what you build. It's what you leave others strong enough to carry.

From The Field To The Boardroom

Tanzania reminded me that leadership isn't always about directing—sometimes it's about witnessing. On safari, the best guides weren't the ones constantly talking; they were the ones who knew when to point something out and when to let us take it in for ourselves. They trusted the environment to teach us what words couldn't.

Organizations thrive in the same way. A leader's role isn't to narrate every move or solve every problem in real time. It's to create conditions where the team can observe, learn, and adapt on their own. The best leaders know when to step forward with direction and when to step back and let the moment shape the people in it.

In the Serengeti, timing was everything. We learned quickly that moving too fast meant missing the lions camouflaged in the grass, while lingering too long meant missing the migration further ahead. In business, the same is true—strategy isn't just about knowing what to do; it's knowing when to move.

TANZANIA:
Leadership Lessons in Visibility and Balance

- Visibility is not vulnerability. Leadership is not just about showing up for others—it's also about allowing yourself to be seen, fully and without apology.

- Excellence isn't always empowerment. When driven by fear, it becomes armor. True empowerment comes from alignment, not overcompensation.

- Rest is not a reward. In nature—and in leadership—rest is strategic. It's what allows systems to regenerate and thrive.

- Legacy is stewardship, not ego. Leadership should honor the past and build for the future. What we create must be designed to outlast us—and uplift others.

- Balance is the real flex. The most enduring systems in nature don't dominate—they harmonize. Our organizations should be no different.

- The next chapter isn't built by pushing harder. It's built by returning—to what matters, to what sustains, to what will last.

PLACES THAT HELD ME IN TANZANIA AND ZANZIBAR

The Arusha Coffee Lodge—a place that intentionally slowed me down, and being inside nature. A threshold space sitting at the edge between arrival and adventure.

Sanctuary Swala Camp—a place that literally put me inside the rhythm of life, with elephants moving past my tent as if I were incidental. It didn't explain itself. It allowed mystery.

The Cultural Heritage Centre—a space that held history with confidence, honoring lineage, craftsmanship, and memory.

Sunset cruise on a dhow—this is where the wind decided the pace, the sunset decided the ending, and we simply followed.

AFRICA

Chapter 5: Legacy in Tanzania

CHAPTER 6

CHAOS AS CLARITY IN CAIRO

I didn't know it when I boarded the plane to Cairo, but something in me had shifted. Not in a flashy way. Not the kind of change you can post about or package. But in the quiet places—the ones that no longer needed to prove, perform, or explain.

I wasn't the same woman who had left home. And I wasn't trying to go back to her, either.

Now, in this in-between—the layover between continents, between versions of myself—I started to notice the integration. I didn't feel the need to fill silence in conversations. I stopped apologizing for choosing rest over hustle. And for the first time in years, I allowed stillness to mean something. Not absence. But presence.

This wasn't the end of the journey. But it was the beginning of leadership reimagined—from the inside out. Not leading to prove. Not leading to protect. But leading to align. To serve. To sustain.

The flight map blinked on. Another leg of the journey awaited. But this time, I wasn't chasing clarity. I was carrying it.

I didn't need the next destination to change me. I just wanted to see what would happen if I stopped trying to direct the journey.

After Tanzania and Zanzibar, I needed a break—but not the kind that required more soul-searching. I needed noise, chaos, distraction. Cairo delivered that instantly. It wasn't asking me to transform. It wasn't holding up a mirror. It simply let me exist inside the swirl of its contradictions—the horns, the dust, the heat, the perpetual motion.

There's a moment in every journey where movement quiets and integration begins. Where you stop pushing for clarity and start noticing what's already changed.

Cairo became that moment for me—not because it was peaceful, but because it didn't demand anything. In the freedom of not having to "heal," I began to recognize the parts of me that already had.

The chaos greeted me from the moment I stepped foot off the plane. It was like nothing I've ever seen before. Thank goodness I had a guide who knew exactly where to find me. He escorted me out of the airport. As I looked at the lines and chaos at the terminal, the guide instantly became my best friend. His name was George. As I entered his car, he warned me there are no lines on the highway in Cairo, that people just drive. Even if there are lines on the highway, they are ignored. Just close your eyes and enjoy what you are about to experience.

Cairo was chaos—beautiful, disorienting chaos. The first notes I noticed were the horns—blaring, insistent, and oddly rhythmic, like a language all their own. Every so often, the deep, resonant call to prayer would float above the din, stretching across the city like a pause in the noise. It wasn't just sound—it was a vibration, a reminder that even in constant motion, there are moments to stop, bow, and acknowledge something larger than ourselves.

By the Nile at sunset, the smell shifted—less exhaust, more water and wind, with a faint trace of something metallic, like stone cooling after a long day in the sun. In the mornings, the air felt heavier, thick with heat and dust that clung to your skin. The city's pulse didn't rise and fall with the clock; morning and night carried the same undercurrent of motion.

Men stood in clusters along sidewalks, hands gesturing animatedly, voices low and rapid, entirely absorbed in each other. I moved through their world as if invisible—an observer in a city that seemed to run just fine without my presence or participation. No one rushed to accommodate me, no one asked what I needed. Cairo wasn't trying to perform for me. It was simply being itself.

And yet, somehow, its apparent disorder worked. Highways without lanes—or maybe lanes that people simply chose to ignore—still flowed. A camel wove through traffic like a secondhand car. People in business attire stood along the highway waiting for their ride to work, as unconcerned by the chaos as if they were standing in a quiet park. At first, it felt anarchic, but the longer I watched, the more I realized there was an unspoken choreography to it all. Cars and people adjusted in real time, making space without formal signals.

In leadership, I've learned that not all systems are visible. What looks like disorder from the outside can be an elegant structure built on trust, instinct, and adaptability. Leaders often try to control every variable, but sometimes the best results come when you let the system breathe—when you trust that people will find their way through. Cairo was proof of that.

One evening, I decided on a sunset cruise along the Nile. The dock was just across the street from my hotel—an easy walk, or so I thought. But in Cairo, crossing the street wasn't just a task; it felt like a ritual. The hotel's concierge team, attuned to the city's rhythm, took on the role of guides for this daily rite. Not a driver. Not security. Just a quiet, streetwise man who took one look at the relentless stream of traffic and said calmly, "Stay close. Walk when I nod."

I stood at the curb as cars surged from every direction, unbothered by lanes or logic. It was like standing at the edge of a river with no bridge—only belief. He gave the nod.

And somehow—miraculously—the cars parted just enough. I moved with him, instinctively, like we'd rehearsed it. It wasn't graceful, but it was sacred. A parting of the Red Sea in rush-hour Cairo.

As chaotic as it appeared, the city seemed to thrive in what looked like dysfunction. Beneath the surface was a complex interplay of formal and informal systems, sustained by an adaptable population that had learned to navigate daily challenges with resourcefulness. I couldn't help but see the parallel to adaptive leadership—where people innovate and find solutions when top-down systems falter.

When I finally reached the other side, heart pounding and breath short, I realized: Sometimes the crossing *is* the story. The sunset was stunning, but it was that street—that chaos, that surrender—that stayed with me. In leadership, as in life, the bravest move isn't always charging forward. Sometimes, it's trusting the guide who knows the rhythm better than you do.

The next day brought a different kind of performance.

I had booked a "flying dress" photo shoot, imagining windswept magic at the foot of the pyramids. Instead, I was met by a silent guide who said nothing about where we were going. We entered a building and began to climb. One flight. Two. Then three. By the time we reached the eighth flight of narrow stairs, I was sweaty, winded, and confused. Only then did we step out onto a rooftop.

The pyramid in the background was real—but the desert illusion was not. Drapes were pinned, fans were positioned, and the entire scene was manufactured. While I stood there holding my pose, I glanced out at the neighboring rooftops and saw a goat casually roaming around, chewing at something near a satellite dish.

It made me laugh. Not the staged illusion—the goat. This strange, feral creature in the middle of the skyline, unaware it didn't belong. Or maybe it did. In Cairo, the rules didn't apply in the same way. Nothing was quite where it should be, and somehow that felt … okay.

On another day, I stood before the Sphinx. Smaller than I had imagined, but still majestic, enigmatic. Part lion, part human, entirely unreadable. The longer I looked at it, the more I felt its silence. It didn't ask to be interpreted. It simply was. Timeless. Worn by sand and time but still standing.

There was also something beneath the surface of the city I couldn't quite name. Guards were stationed everywhere—at hotels, historical sites, even outside casual restaurants. Men with rifles stood casually near tourist paths. They chatted easily with each other, as if this, too, was just part of daily life. And maybe it was. Egypt seemed to be holding something tense beneath its surface, like a city trying to breathe through a tight chest.

And yet, I never felt threatened. Not once. Surprised, often. Disoriented, frequently. But not unsafe. Maybe that's what happens when your nervous system has already been stretched by your own internal unrest—you stop flinching at the external sort.

In the middle of all this contradiction, I visited the newly opened Grand Egyptian Museum. Over 100,000 artifacts—many dating back more than 4,500 years—housed under one sleek, modern roof. It was staggering. The gold, the hieroglyphs, the silent presence of civilizations that once ruled the known world. It was a museum, yes, but it was also a message: We've always been trying to make sense of things. To preserve what matters. To give shape to chaos through stories carved in stone.

As I was leaving, I passed a large statue inscribed in block letters: **BUILT FOR ETERNITY.** It stopped me in my tracks. It made me think about leadership. Building sustainable organizations doesn't mean they won't be tested. *Built for Eternity* means the structure, the foundation, and the *why* are so deeply embedded that they permeate every decision, every process, and every person. That depth allows an organization to adapt without losing its identity.

Cairo's streets proved it: Resilience isn't about resisting change—it's about knowing your rhythm so well that even in chaos, you keep moving forward. In leadership, that means creating cultures that can improvise without losing themselves.

That was the message of Egypt. Even in the chaos. Even through conquest, colonization, and collapse. Still, the artifacts remain. Still, the structures stand. Still, the stories live.

Cairo didn't give me clarity. It didn't stir deep revelations or pull trauma to the surface. What it gave me was a reprieve. A surreal, sometimes absurd, slightly off-kilter place to just exist without meaning-making. No healing. No transformation. Just a moment to be in a place where things didn't always make sense—and where that, somehow, was a relief.

Because even the most chaotic places can leave behind something eternal.

FROM THE FIELD TO THE BOARDROOM

Egypt was a lesson in navigating complexity with grace. Cairo's streets moved like a living organism—no clear lanes, no obvious order, yet somehow everyone flowed. It wasn't chaos for chaos's sake; it was an unspoken system built on awareness, adaptability, and trust in one another's instincts.

In leadership, the same applies. Not every environment is going to be orderly or predictable. The real skill is learning to operate within complexity without forcing it into shapes it was never meant to take. A rigid leader tries to control every variable. An adaptive leader learns to move with the current while keeping the destination in sight.

Egypt also showed me the power of legacy in shaping the present. The pyramids, temples, and monuments weren't just relics—they were living symbols of what's possible when vision meets perseverance. In organizations, vision without endurance fades quickly; endurance without vision becomes stagnation. The magic is in holding both.

CAIRO:
LEADERSHIP LESSONS IN CHAOS AND CONTINUITY

Find rhythm in the disorder. Cairo's streets looked chaotic, but beneath the noise was an unspoken choreography—people adjusting, responding, and flowing in real time. Reminds me of a leadership lesson I learned watching jazz ensembles. Trust at work.

Trust the guide. Crossing a Cairo street required surrender—moving in rhythm with someone who knew the pattern better than I did. Leadership isn't always about leading from the front; sometimes it's about trusting others to set the pace, watching for the nod, and moving together through uncertainty.

Authenticity over illusion. The "flying dress" shoot at the pyramids was a study in performance—fans, drapes, and the illusion of perfection. The goat on the rooftop reminded me of what realness looks like. Leadership doesn't require staging certainty. The courage to show up unscripted is what builds trust.

Build for endurance, not applause. Egypt's monuments were *Built for Eternity*—not just constructed but conceived to last. True leadership is the same. It's about embedding purpose so deeply that the organization endures beyond personalities, market cycles, or crises. Legacy is built in the foundation, not the spotlight.

Stillness amid motion. Cairo didn't offer calm; it offered movement that never stopped. Yet, within that constant motion, there were moments of pause—the call to prayer, the quiet of the Nile at dusk. Leadership, too, requires finding stillness within chaos—space to breathe, observe, and realign before acting.

PLACES THAT HELD ME IN EGYPT

The Nile River—A current of contrast; chaos at its edges, calm at its center. It held my surrender, reminding me that flow doesn't need direction to have purpose.

The streets of Cairo—Honking, pulsing, alive. They held the rhythm of adaptation—proof that even in disorder, people find their way through instinct and awareness.

The Grand Egyptian Museum—A modern vessel for ancient wisdom. It held the endurance of humanity's story—our collective desire to preserve what matters, even when everything changes.

The Sphinx—Silent and steadfast, weathered but unbroken. It held mystery—a reminder that not all things are meant to be explained, and not every question requires an answer.

The Pyramids of Giza—Precision carved in permanence. They held the awe of endurance—how vision, aligned with purpose, can transcend time itself.

The rooftops of Cairo—Where illusion and authenticity met—a staged desert, a wandering goat, and a quiet laugh. They held perspective—the grace of finding truth in imperfection.

The call to prayer—Rising above the noise, rhythmic and grounding. It held reverence—the pause between motion, the moment that asks you to bow to something larger than yourself.

The crossing at the Nile street—That ordinary, heart-pounding moment of trust. It held humility—the lesson that leadership sometimes means letting someone else lead you through.

Built for Eternity

○

EXHALING IN SWITZERLAND

> *To depart is not always to escape—*
> *sometimes, it is to evolve.*
> *—Myrna Lamarque*

Like Egypt before it, Switzerland wasn't part of any grand plan. It was simply a yes to something I'd always wanted to do, to visit the Montreux Jazz Festival. No deeper motive. No transformation agenda. Just beauty. Just rhythm. Just stillness. Montreux in July is a city that hums. The air along Lake Geneva feels charged, as if the music seeps into the water itself. I hadn't realized how long it had been since I let joy exist for its own sake—without turning it into purpose, meaning, or productivity.

Switzerland was all soft light and green hills, shimmering lakes and delicate order. A kind of peacefulness that didn't have to prove anything. After the absurd choreography of Cairo's streets, Switzerland felt like finally releasing the breath I didn't know I was holding.

Switzerland unfolded like a painting come to life—mountains mirrored in glassy lakes, villages tucked neatly between valleys, trains gliding with quiet precision. There was a stillness to it, but not an emptiness—more like a country completely at peace with its own rhythm.

Switzerland felt like balance made visible. Even its languages—German, French, and Italian—flowed together without denying their differences, as naturally as its lakes and valleys. It reminded me that harmony isn't sameness; it's the art of allowing contrast to live side by side with it—a truth I was only beginning to practice within myself.

That balance seemed to extend beyond the landscape—it lived in the people too.

One afternoon, while riding the bus from Vevey to Montreux, I must have looked completely lost. I wasn't sure if I'd paid correctly or even if I was heading in the right direction. A woman seated nearby noticed my hesitation and leaned over with a gentle smile. "Do you need help?" she asked. Her tone was kind, not curious—the kind of kindness that offers safety without expectation.

We started talking—two strangers sharing fragments of our lives between stops. There was an ease about her that felt both grounding and familiar. And then, almost without thinking, I asked, "Would it be all right if I visited your home? I'd love to see how people really live here."

She laughed softly, surprised but not at all put off. "Of course," she said. "Come tomorrow."

Only later did I learn how extraordinary that "yes" really was. After I got off the bus, she called her husband.

"I just did the most random thing," she told him. "I invited a complete stranger to our home."

Instead of alarm, there was laughter. Curiosity. When she shared the story with her family, their response surprised me even more—they were delighted. Excited. As if the unexpectedness of it all had added something bright to an otherwise ordinary day.

Thank you, Géraldine, I thought. For the trust. For the openness. For reminding me that sometimes joy enters not through intention, but through an unguarded yes.

The next day, I did something I might never have done before: I went.

Her home sat high on a hill, overlooking a sweep of green hills and mountains. Through wide windows, I could see the world folded below—tidy roads, mirrored lakes, the faint shimmer of Lake Geneva in the distance. Inside, everything was immaculate but inviting—modern lines, gleaming surfaces, sunlight pooling across polished floors. It was precision and warmth in perfect balance, much like Switzerland itself.

We drank coffee and spoke about ordinary things—family, work, the small joys of everyday life. There was no pretense, no exchange of numbers, no future plan. Just people sharing space and quiet understanding.

As I walked back down the hill later that day, I looked out over the lake and realized that this was what peace looked like—not the absence of movement, but the ease that comes from trusting the moment you're in. In another season of my life, I would have hesitated—overthinking, protecting, performing. But here, surrounded by balance and grace, I said yes.

Maybe that's what stillness really is—not the absence of motion, but the courage to move gently toward what's unfamiliar.

That night, as the lights of Montreux reflected on Lake Geneva, I found myself surrounded by another kind of language—music.

The jazz singer Celeste opened the evening with a set so intimate it felt like she was singing to each of us individually. I'd never heard of her before, but the minute she started singing, I found myself pulling out my phone to look her up. Her voice and style reminded me of both Amy Winehouse and Lady Gaga—soulful yet theatrical, vulnerable yet commanding. There was a quiet electricity in the air as she performed, the kind that asks you to stop talking, stop scrolling, and just *listen*.

And then, as night settled over Lake Geneva, Lionel Richie took the stage. I had to pause—not just in the moment, but in my own mind. This was Lionel Richie: a legend whose music had been the soundtrack to so many seasons of my life. I grew up on his voice—the one that could fill a stadium yet somehow feel like it was singing just to you. For over fifty years, he's stood the test of time, crossing generations and genres without losing the heart in his sound.

Here he was, right in front of me, his voice as smooth and effortless as the first time I heard him through my parents' record player. It wasn't nostalgia—it was *continuity.* Proof that some artistry doesn't fade with age; it deepens. Every lyric, every note carried the weight of decades and the joy of someone who still loves what they do. The crowd sang with him—strangers linked by memory, melody, and that rare magic that happens when music bypasses the brain and goes straight to the soul.

Standing there, I realized it wasn't just about hearing a legend; it was about witnessing endurance—joy, mastery, and the kind of purpose that outlives applause.

During the day, the music spilled into the streets—free concerts at every turn, the air threaded with saxophone riffs, bass lines, and voices that didn't need microphones to be heard. I wandered from stage to stage, letting curiosity dictate my steps. No plan. No urgency. Just music, the lake, and the hum of a city alive in every direction.

During our stay one morning, we took a two-hour scenic drive from Vevey, winding past tidy villages and wildflower-strewn pastures, heading toward waterfalls and gorges I had never heard of. Our first stop was Reichenbach Falls—a towering cascade made famous by Sherlock Holmes's final showdown with Moriarty. A funicular lifted us to the top, gliding steadily up the slope as the falls roared beside us. The view from the summit was commanding, cinematic. I stood there for a long time, doing nothing but watching the water crash below. And for once, that was enough. I didn't need to extract meaning from it. Just being there was the meaning.

Later that afternoon, I did something I never imagined myself doing: I hiked. The infamous Aare Gorge, where narrow walkways snake between sheer rock faces and the sound of rushing water echoes like a heartbeat in the geology of the Alps. The path clung to the cliffs—elevated, winding, exposed. At one point, I looked down and realized I was face-to-face with one of my quiet fears: heights.

I toughened up and it felt strong. Not the kind of strength that comes from training or preparation, but the kind that appears when you decide, without fanfare, that you're just going to keep going.

Heights had always been a quiet vulnerability for me. They made my pulse quicken, my breath shorten—not from exertion, but from the dizzying awareness of just how far there was to fall. Yet that day, I didn't ask how high the climb would be or how far the trail stretched ahead. I didn't need to.

From the moment I stepped onto the path, I became mesmerized by the gushing waters. The sound was constant, insistent, almost hypnotic. It pulled my focus away from the drop beside me and anchored it in something steady and alive. The path wound along sheer rock faces, elevated walkways clinging to the cliffs, the air cool and damp from the spray. At times, the ground seemed to vanish just inches from where I placed my feet, but instead of tightening, my body loosened.

Each step felt like an act of quiet defiance—not against the fear itself, but against the reflex to retreat from it. I didn't conquer my fear of heights that day; I moved with it. It was there, humming in the background, but it didn't dictate my pace or my presence.

Standing there in Switzerland, fresh from the roar of the falls—water crashing, mist rising—a memory flashed back to me.

On my last day in Tokyo, I realized I was carrying too much. Not just in my suitcase—but in my spirit. I went to the post office and shipped two boxes home. And even then, I was intentional: what I needed for the very next destination always went into my carry-on—essentials, important pieces—just in case my luggage was lost. It was strategy. It was self-trust mixed with self-protection. A woman learning to release … but not abandon herself.

In South Korea, I shipped more home. By then it wasn't difficult—it felt freeing.

And by the time I arrived in Switzerland, I couldn't even remember what I had sent back. I didn't care if those boxes ever arrived. That was the proof—the release had already happened. Somewhere between Tokyo, Seoul, and these Swiss falls … I became lighter.

In leadership, I had spent years mastering control—predicting outcomes, removing uncertainty, minimizing risk. But here, in this gorge carved over millennia, I didn't control anything. I just kept moving forward, breath by breath, step by step. And in that surrender, I found something unexpected: ease.

When the trail finally opened into a wider vista, I stopped. The river rushed below, foaming white against the dark stone, the sound filling every corner of the space. I stood there, unhurried, no need to get anywhere else. The fear was still there—but so was I.

And here's the thing: I didn't stop. I didn't panic. I kept going.

It was exhilarating. Not because I conquered anything, but because I allowed myself to move through fear without judgment.

Later, we hiked again—this time through the lush trails leading to Giessbach Falls. If the Aare Gorge was about moving with fear, Giessbach Falls was about letting go of it altogether.

The trail here was softer, shaded by tall trees that filtered the light into a gentle green glow. The air carried the scent of moss and wet earth, and somewhere ahead, the falls announced themselves—not with the insistent roar of the gorge's river, but with a steady, rhythmic cascade.

As I followed the winding path, I felt no urgency. My steps matched the slow sway of branches overhead, the occasional burst of birdsong, the quiet conversations of hikers passing by. The sound of the falls grew louder, but instead of pulling me forward like the gorge had, it seemed to draw me inward.

When I finally reached the base, water arced from the cliff in a perfect, continuous sweep before crashing into the pool below. Mist drifted into the air, settling lightly on my skin. There was no fear here, no edge to negotiate—just the steady, unbroken flow of something much older and more certain than me.

I stood for a long time, not to take the perfect photo or check another destination off a list, but to notice what happened when I stopped moving. The world didn't end. The trail didn't vanish. And for perhaps the first time in my career and my travels, I didn't feel the pull to manage the moment.

If the gorge had taught me that I could keep going even with fear in my pocket, Giessbach taught me that sometimes strength comes from setting the pocket down altogether. From letting the current, the mist, and the moment hold you—no striving required.

This became the quiet magic of Switzerland: It gave me both. A chance to test my edges, and a place to lay them down.

Before leaving Switzerland, I visited Château de Chillon—perched on the edge of Lake Geneva like something out of a fairy tale. It was stunning. Majestic. Storybook on the outside, with snowcapped mountains behind it and a glassy lake below. But once inside, I felt a shift. The beauty gave way to shadows. Stone walls. Cold air. Echoes of captivity.

Built in the 11th century by the House of Savoy, the château once guarded a narrow trade route between northern and southern Europe. Centuries later, it became a prison, its dungeons carved into the rock below the waterline. One of its most famous captives, François Bonivard—a Genevan monk and political dissident—was chained to a pillar for six years. His story inspired

Lord Byron's *The Prisoner of Chillon,* a poem about endurance, spirit, and freedom that refuses to be broken.

The deeper we walked into the chambers, the more the silence thickened. Dungeons. Chains. The carved initials of prisoners trying to mark their place in time. There was something haunting about it. How a place so breathtaking could hold so much sorrow. How light and darkness could live in the same space.

I stood at the edge of a window slit—where someone long ago might have stood, watching the lake but unable to reach it—and thought: This is also what it means to evolve. To hold beauty and pain in the same breath. To see the joy without looking away from the grief. To know that the view isn't always the full story.

It felt like a mirror for every leader who's ever had to smile through the weight of what they couldn't say aloud.

And maybe that's not just true of Switzerland—or history. Maybe it's true of the present. Of where I live now. Because even in the polished corridors of power, in the relentless pursuit of influence and wealth, there's a similar duality. Light and darkness. Beauty and distortion. Moments of awe, and systems of harm. And without grounding—without reflection—it's easy to forget which one you're serving.

Switzerland taught me to rest. But Chillon reminded me that even in rest, there is reckoning.

And maybe that's the lesson Switzerland offered me, without ever saying a word: You don't always have to climb your way into peace. Sometimes, it waits for you. Quietly. Gently. On the other side of permission.

FROM THE FIELD
TO THE BOARDROOM

Switzerland reminded me that stillness is not the absence of movement—it's the presence of intention. Whether it was the hum of the Montreux Jazz Festival or the quiet force of waterfalls and mountain trails, I learned that pace matters. Not everything worth building is born from urgency; some of the most enduring outcomes emerge from spaces where presence outweighs productivity.

Hiking narrow cliffside paths over the Aare Gorge taught me something about leadership vulnerability. I didn't ask how far or how high; I simply started walking. In organizations, we often overanalyze risks until momentum dies. Sometimes, the right move is to step forward without needing every answer—to trust the path and adjust as you go.

The Château de Chillon added another layer: Beauty and darkness can live side by side. In leadership, as in history, we can't romanticize the wins without also acknowledging the shadows. Strong leaders hold space for both—celebrating progress while confronting the uncomfortable truths that remain.

SWITZERLAND:
LEADERSHIP LESSONS IN STILLNESS AND STRENGTH

- Stillness is strategic—Pausing is not wasted time; it's a recalibration that sharpens focus. It can be just as powerful as decisive actions.

- Lead through uncertainty—You don't need perfect information to take the first step.

- Honor complexity—True leadership means recognizing both the triumphs and the shadows of an organization's story. In leadership, acknowledging the darker realities alongside the wins builds credibility and trust. Great leaders can celebrate success without ignoring the struggles that came with it. This dual awareness helps ground decision-making in reality rather than optics.

- Presence over productivity—Sometimes the most impactful leadership happens when you stop managing and start listening.

- Strength can come from surrender.

Giessbach Falls embodied the leadership truth that power can come from letting go. Not every situation demands control or intervention. Knowing when to release the need to manage every detail allows others to step in, creativity to flourish, and the leader to rest—preventing burnout and enabling longevity.

PLACES THAT HELD ME IN SWITZERLAND

Staubbach Falls: Free-falling water like a ribbon of light, reminding me that release can be both powerful and graceful.

Giessbach Falls: Cascading terraces above Lake Brienz, each level slowing the descent, teaching me that nothing has to rush.

Lake Geneva: Wide, elegant, and reflective, holding on to stillness the way a mirror holds truth.

Montreux: Lakefront calm that would invite breath back to my body.

Châteaux de Chillon: Stone, history, and silence that are layered together, holding centuries without the need to speak.

Chapter 7: Exhaling in Switzerland

MONTREUX JAZZ
FESTIVAL 4-19 JULY 2025

MONTReuX
Jazz Festival

Chapter 7: Exhaling in Switzerland

———— o ————

ANCESTRAL MEMORY IN GHANA

> " Some stories don't begin
> —they return. "

There's a point in every journey where the path stops feeling like escape and begins to feel like return. Not a return to what was, but to what's always been waiting: ancestry, intuition, wholeness.

At this point, I no longer needed the distance to see clearly. The places I had visited—their silence, their rituals, their contradictions—had done their work. I had unraveled, integrated, softened. But I hadn't yet rerooted.

Ghana wasn't just another stop. It was a moment of internal reordering. A reclamation. After months of traveling outward, this was a journey inward—a return to the roots of legacy, identity, and history that run deeper than any one leader, role, or organization. So deep, it couldn't be intellectualized—only felt. It reminded me that leadership isn't just forward-facing. It's backward-reaching, too. It honors the shoulders we stand on.

During my visit, I stood before the final resting places of visionaries: the W.E.B. Du Bois Memorial Centre, where a legacy of Pan-Africanism still pulses quietly through the air, and the Kwame Nkrumah Mausoleum—a monument to a man who helped shape the independence of a continent. These weren't just landmarks. They were living reminders of what it means to build for something beyond the self.

The afternoon sun in Accra was heavy, its heat pressing down as I stepped onto the grounds of the Kwame Nkrumah Memorial Centre. The marble walkway gleamed, and the fountains whispered softly in the background, but what lingered most was the silence—a silence that seemed to carry the weight of a nation's story. Here rested Nkrumah, the man who dared to dream of an Africa free, united, and proud.

He was more than Ghana's first president; he was the spark that ignited a continent. Educated abroad, he returned home with a vision so fierce that it shook colonial rule to its core. In 1957, when Ghana declared independence, he stood before the world and proclaimed that Ghana's freedom would mean nothing unless it was bound to the liberation of all Africa. His words still echo in the stone, in the air, in the faces of those who pass through this place.

As I moved through the memorial, I felt the duality of his legacy—the grandeur of his vision and the weight of its imperfections. He built schools, factories, roads; he called for unity that stretched beyond borders. Yet his rule tightened, opposition grew, and in 1966, while abroad, he was stripped of power. Exiled until his death, he never walked these streets again. Still, his presence lingers, woven into the pride of Ghana and the memory of a continent.

Later, at the W.E.B. Du Bois Memorial Centre, the air felt equally sacred. Here lay the scholar who had carried the struggle of Black liberation across oceans and decades, who in his final years answered Nkrumah's call to make Ghana his home. Their lives converged here, on this soil—Africa and her diaspora bound together in vision, sacrifice, and hope.

At one of the local naming ceremonies, I was reminded just how deeply identity is honored here. In Ghana, the day you are born carries its own name and character—not as a label, but as a calling. This practice comes from the Akan, one of the country's largest ethnic groups, where each day of the week traditionally corresponds to a spiritual identity and set of attributes believed to shape one's destiny.

I was born on a Friday: Afua. The name felt both familiar and new, like a thread I had been holding all along without knowing its origin. In Akan belief, Friday-born women are known for creativity, nurturing strength, and leadership.

Hearing this, I felt a spark of recognition. Those qualities weren't assigned to me that day—they had *always* been present.

Leading teams through uncertainty, creating space for others to thrive, and now, daring to reinvent myself at sixty. Afua wasn't simply a name; it was a mirror, reflecting back who I had always been.

Later, when I returned to the grave of W.E.B. Du Bois, I thought of that name again. Du Bois had also chosen a new identity in Ghana—a final act of belonging to something larger than himself. Even at ninety-three, he was still willing to uproot and begin again. In that choice, I recognized the same truth Afua whispered to me: that creativity and courage are not limited by age.

I carried that lesson with me as I walked away from the memorial. A name and a legacy—both reminders that we are always free to begin again, to create anew, and to lead in ways that align with who we truly are.

Standing between these two memorials, I felt a stirring inside me. Both men had devoted themselves to something larger than their own lives, knowing their work might remain unfinished. And I, too, had come to Ghana seeking renewal— carrying the ache of a chapter I had left behind, searching for the courage to begin again. In the stillness, I understood reinvention is never easy, but it is always possible. Sometimes the most radical act is simply to rise, to reimagine, and to claim your own freedom story.

From there, I made my way to Black Star Square—the heart of Accra and Ghana's monument to independence, vision, and possibility. Standing beneath the black star, the symbol of African freedom and unity, I felt a weight and a widening at the same time. It was more than stone and sky; it was a declaration. A reminder that liberation is both collective and personal. Here, Ghana had claimed its own voice. And in that moment, I felt the faint echo of my own—rising, steady, refusing to shrink. Legacy wasn't an abstract idea anymore. It was something you could stand inside of.

The next day, I traveled to the Slave River—the place where captured Africans were forced to bathe before being sold. No textbook could have prepared me for the quiet devastation of that water. The river moved gently, as if trying to reconcile the memories it carried. I stepped into it, letting the current wrap around my ankles.

And I wept. Not just for them. But for every way I had ever tried to prove I belonged in spaces that were never built for me.

The water held centuries of grief, but it also held resilience. It was the beginning of erasure for those who passed through it—but standing there, it became the beginning of remembrance for me.

From the river, I traveled to Cape Coast Castle, and the shift was immediate—from open sky to heavy stone, from flowing water to suffocating walls. I walked through the dungeons carved into the earth, places where men, women, and children were held in darkness, in silence, in unimaginable dehumanization. Above those dungeons stood a church—a chilling reminder of how violence and righteousness once shared a roof.

The dissonance was staggering. Prayers above. Screams below. A theology built on selective sight.

I stood at the Door of No Return—the portal through which millions passed, robbed of name, land, lineage, and future. And yet, the ocean beyond that door glimmered with light, as if refusing to let the story end in darkness.

Standing in that threshold, I felt history press into me. Not to crush, but to clarify.

That evening, I found myself on the rooftop of Skybar—one of Accra's most vibrant, electric spaces—overlooking a city alive with light, music, and possibility. The contrast was staggering. Hours earlier, I had stood in a place carved by sorrow; now I stood above a city pulsing with joy and forward movement. It reminded me that Ghana is not one story—it is multiplicity. Grief and celebration. Memory and momentum. A place held together by both what it has endured and what it insists on becoming.

Ghana taught me that legacy is layered. It's pain, yes—but also pride. It's resistance and reverence. It's the fire that keeps burning even after centuries of attempts to extinguish it.

Standing there, I felt the weight of both history and healing. I felt connected to something ancient, something resilient. And for the first time in a long time, I didn't feel like I had to earn my place. And that reminder? It changed everything.

In Ghana, I was given a name—not as a title, but as a recognition. **Afua Serwaa Agyeman.** A name rooted in calm, stewardship, and responsibility to what comes next.

Because of time, we did not move through the full naming ceremony. Instead, the ritual was explained—the meaning laid out carefully, intentionally. I was told how, in the complete ceremony, water would touch the tongue to remind the bearer that voice carries consequence—that leadership begins not in volume, but in truth. An offering would be made to the earth, so the name would be anchored not just in sound, but in place—in lineage, responsibility, and belonging.

Even without every step enacted, the meaning landed. I didn't feel changed; I felt *aligned*. I wasn't becoming someone new. I was reclaiming the authority to speak, to lead, and to stand fully present without shrinking.

And in that moment, I understood something clearly: Leadership is not something you claim. It is something you are entrusted with—once you remember who you are.

There's a saying: If you don't know where you're from, you don't know where you're going. Ghana made that real for me. In a world where so many are consumed by work—chasing titles, metrics, and milestones without meaning—Ghana reminded me that understanding your roots is not a luxury. It's a necessity. Knowing what shaped you, what drives you, and what you carry gives depth to everything you build. It gives leadership clarity, a company its soul, and legacy its pulse.

The air carried stories of resilience and ingenuity—of those who built pathways where none existed. Progress, I realized, is rarely a solo act. It's the accumulation of effort, sacrifice, and vision from those who came before us. In leadership, organizations grow the same way. Every milestone rests on a foundation laid by others—mentors, predecessors, and quiet contributors who paved the way.

Truth calls us to do more than just lead in the present. It calls us to reach back—to train and develop those within our care so they can carry the mission forward. True leadership is legacy work. It is honoring the past not simply through remembrance, but by creating the conditions for others to build upon it—ensuring the future stands taller because we stood together in the present.

In my own leadership journey—from scaling organizations to guiding teams through transition—I've seen how often legacy is treated as an afterthought, when in fact it should be the starting point.

Ghana connected me to humanity. It reminded me that, no matter where we are in the world, we're part of a much larger puzzle. Our roles, our businesses, our ambitions—they don't exist in a vacuum. They're part of something collective. Something sacred.

And in that realization, I understood something even deeper: My purpose is far greater than just me. These weren't just destinations on a map—they were portals. Each site opened something in me and closed something else. In Ghana, I didn't just remember. I re-membered—putting myself back together, piece by piece, with clarity, courage, and connection.

One of the most striking aspects of my time in Ghana was the warmth with which I was received. Whether in a formal setting or walking through a market, people greeted me with a kind of grounded hospitality—open, proud, and deeply human. There is a quiet dignity in people here, a genuine pride in who they are and where they come from. It's not performative. It's cultural. It's ancestral.

That pride—that presence—reminded me of something every organization must understand: Culture isn't built through mission statements. It's built through how people show up.

Ghana showed me that when people feel connected to identity, to community, to legacy—they lead differently. They serve differently. They build differently.

It left me wondering: What would it look like if our companies operated from that same sense of belonging? What might be possible if pride in purpose wasn't something we had to force, but something we simply lived?

I couldn't help but think back to moments in my career when leadership missed the mark on what truly inspires people. Times when, instead of leaning into connection and trust, the focus shifted to optics—trying to curate an image rather than address the heart of the issue. I've seen organizations respond to employee dissatisfaction not by listening, but by orchestrating campaigns of self-promotion—asking leaders to collect glowing testimonials or showcase symbols of success as if that would erase deeper concerns.

The truth is, when people are rooted in who they are and are connected to a shared purpose, you don't have to convince them to be proud of where they work. Pride becomes performance—not from pressure, but from purpose. And once you've seen the difference, you start spotting the gap everywhere.

That kind of leadership doesn't just produce outcomes. It creates cultures that last—and workplaces that people want to stay in.

In Ghana, I saw that words carried more weight than wealth. Dignity, trust, and legacy were the true currency. And when people feel seen, valued, and proud—you don't need to overcompensate with bonuses or perks. You build loyalty through belonging.

What Ghana gave me was not a loud revelation, but a quiet shift—a deeper knowing of where I stand and who I stand with. It wasn't something I planned to take with me, but it traveled anyway, threading itself into the way I would move through the rest of my journey. Once you've felt the weight and gift of standing on the shoulders of giants, you never see the world the same way again.

Every place after Ghana carried a different texture, a different meaning—as if I was walking not just for myself, but with the echoes of those who came before me. That weight didn't slow me down; it grounded me. It reminded me that joy, connection, and even adventure can be acts of honoring the past.

Which is why, when I arrived in Colombia, I was ready for something entirely different—a country that met me with vibrancy, rhythm, and a pulse that demanded I step fully into the present.

From the Field to the Boardroom

Ghana reminded me that leadership is never built in isolation—it's the culmination of everything that came before you. Standing on the shoulders of giants is not just a metaphor; it's a responsibility. The visionaries, risk-takers, and quiet builders who paved the way for progress did so without always seeing the outcome. In organizations, the same is true. Every success is an echo of someone else's effort, whether their name is remembered or not.

In the boardroom, this translates into a simple but powerful truth: Leaders must reach back. Progress doesn't just mean chasing the next milestone—it means ensuring those coming behind you are equipped, empowered, and inspired to carry the mission forward. The work is not finished when the target is hit; it is finished when others are capable of surpassing it.

Ghana also underscored that culture is not a slogan—it is the lived experience of people who feel connected to identity, purpose, and belonging. In Accra and Cape Coast, I saw how pride in heritage naturally shaped behavior, relationships, and collaboration. It wasn't imposed. It was embodied. The same applies to organizations: Culture is not built through quarterly statements or marketing campaigns, but through how leaders show up, day after day, in ways that honor the values they claim to hold.

The corporate world often mistakes performance for purpose, assuming that hitting metrics automatically sustains an organization. But Ghana revealed the reverse—that purpose fuels performance. When people are deeply rooted in meaning, they deliver results with a resilience and creativity that no incentive plan can replicate.

The question I carried home was this: What would it look like if more companies led like Ghana lives? If they measured success not just in quarterly growth, but in how well they preserved dignity, built community, and passed the torch? Because when the next generation stands on your shoulders, the real measure of leadership will be whether they can see farther because you stood here first.

GHANA:
LEADERSHIP LESSONS IN LEGACY AND LINEAGE

Lead with legacy in mind: Enduring leadership isn't measured by short-term wins—it's about building systems and institutions that serve generations beyond your own.

Honor the truth of history: What we refuse to name becomes embedded in our cultures. Reckoning isn't weakness; it's wisdom—the kind that frees us to lead with clarity and integrity.

Reclaim your worth: Leadership rooted in identity doesn't need to perform—it remembers. It stands tall without waiting for permission.

You are enough without proving yourself: Presence. Clarity. Care. These are not rewards for overwork—they are your inheritance.

Grief can be generative: Let loss refine your empathy and deepen your resolve. Leadership isn't only strategic—it's profoundly human.

- Build institutions, not just movements: Vision inspires, but structure sustains. Legacy lives not only in ideas but in the systems that protect and extend them.

- You are the bridge: Leadership is an act of lineage—carrying forward what's sacred while releasing what no longer serves.

Places That Held Me in Ghana

W.E.B. Du Bois Center—A quiet yet powerful archive of Pan-African thought and liberation, housing Du Bois's personal library and final resting place.

Kwame Nkrumah Mausoleum—A monument to Ghana's first president and the spirit of independence, framed by stillness and solemn dignity.

Cape Coast Castle—A place of both horror and remembrance. The Door of No Return will never leave me.

Slave River (Assin Manso)—Where I laid my hands in the water and felt the sorrow, resilience, and memory of generations held in its current.

Black Star Square (Independence Square)—Where I felt the pride of the nation rise beneath my feet.

BLACK STAR SQUARE

WELCOME TO THE ANCESTRAL RIVER PARK

OSAGYEFO
1909 - 1972

FIRST BATH OF RETURN

AD 1957
FREEDOM AND JUSTICE

Chapter 8: Ancestral Memory in Ghana

CHAPTER 9

JOY IN COLOMBIA

By the time I arrived in Colombia, something in me had softened. The urgency to search, to analyze, to name every shift—it had loosened its grip. I wasn't chasing clarity anymore. I was living it. Colombia didn't feel like a continuation of the journey; it felt like a *celebration* of it—in bold, unapologetic color.

The moment I stepped into Cartagena, I felt it in my bones—the rhythm, the pulse, the life that was both ancient and electric. Joy seemed to live in the air itself, dancing through the music that spilled from plazas, coloring the walls with stories too vivid to ignore. The city felt alive in a way that asked nothing of me except to *feel*.

Only later did I fully understand the place that had been holding me.

Inside the walled city stood the Sofitel Legend Santa Clara, where I stayed—a building that had worn many identities across four centuries. Once a convent, then a hospital, and now a luxury hotel, it carried the imprint of every life it had lived. Colonial arches rose above sunlit courtyards, where the scent of jasmine mingled with the cool air drifting off stone walls. Here, devotion, resilience, and reinvention weren't just memories— they were the architecture itself.

Its transformation wasn't about erasing the past, but about honoring it—layering beauty over endurance, joy over survival. In the quiet, you could almost hear the echoes of cloistered footsteps and whispered prayers. Step outside, and life erupted in technicolor—horse-drawn carriages clattering over cobblestones, fruit vendors calling above the crowd, children chasing soccer balls through the plaza. History and the present weren't separate here. They coexisted, breathing the same air—and I loved that.

What surprised me most about Colombia was how *safe* I felt roaming the streets. I wandered alone through narrow alleys lit by lanterns, music spilling from open doors, the air thick with the scent of salt and sweetness. For the first time in a long time, I wasn't scanning for danger or rehearsing exits. I was simply present—unguarded, at ease. *Could it be that I no longer needed to hide?*

That sense of safety stayed with me even as the night slowed. We had dinner reservations at Restaurant 1621, and while waiting, we stopped by the hotel's bar, El Coro. What began as a casual detour unfolded into a quiet revelation. The music was soft, the lighting low, and the air carried the scent of aged stone and wine. Near the back, a discreet staircase led downward into the old convent crypt—where the abbesses of Santa Clara were once laid to rest. The space was cool and hushed, its walls breathing history. You could almost feel the pulse of the past there—the rhythm of prayer, the echo of devotion, the solemn endurance of lives lived in faith and silence.

It was only later that I learned these same walls had once stirred Gabriel García Márquez into writing *Of Love and Other Demons*—a story born from silence, devotion, and lives misunderstood.

Above us, laughter and conversation rose from the courtyard, colliding gently with the murmurs of the past below. The contrast was striking—life moving forward even as the past lingered in the stones. Standing there, I realized that transformation doesn't mean forgetting; it means carrying what came before into what we are becoming. Cartagena taught me that—how beauty and endurance can coexist, how joy can rise out of walls once shaped by sorrow. I didn't realize it then, but that night in the crypt would echo again later, in the most unexpected places.

Walking those corridors later, I felt the echo of my own journey. Transformation rarely means starting over; it means carrying the architecture of your past while letting it be reshaped by what comes next. The walls I once built for protection could also become places where joy and expansion thrive.

That same energy carried me to San Basilio de Palenque—the first free African town in the Americas. Just an hour from Cartagena, yet a world apart, Palenque was founded by escaped enslaved Africans who refused to be broken. They carved out a space of sovereignty and defiance, building a community grounded in self-determination, kinship, and pride long before the world around them recognized their freedom.

Walking through the village felt like stepping into a living archive. History wasn't preserved in stone monuments or museum glass; it pulsed through the beat of the drums and the cadence of the Palenquero language—a language born of resistance and survival. The drums were more than instruments; they were lifelines. Centuries ago, they carried coded messages between settlements, summoning courage, warning of danger, and sustaining connection when spoken words could not. Even now, their rhythms seem to echo that ancient purpose—a steady reminder that communication, in its purest form, is an act of resilience.

I was welcomed into the home of one of the locals, where we shared a meal—simple, homemade, and rich with flavor and history. As we ate, I listened to their stories, feeling the warmth of their hospitality and the quiet pride in their preservation of culture. Watching the children dance and the elders speak, I realized that freedom in Palenque isn't only a legacy—it's a living practice, carried forward in every beat of the drum, every shared meal, every act of resilience.

The women of Palenque, dressed in brightly colored fabrics and balancing baskets of fruit on their heads, were not simply figures of folklore—they were symbols of survival. Of beauty born from struggle. Of joy that refused to be silenced. Everything about Palenque felt like an affirmation: *We are still here. Still thriving. Still free.*

And standing there, surrounded by that energy, I felt something anchor in me.

What surprised me was how quickly that groundedness turned into lightness. The very next day, Colombia invited me into joy in motion.

I took a private boat out across the Caribbean, drifting between three small islands just off the coast, where the water stretched endlessly and time seemed to loosen its grip.

Then, as if summoned, a small wooden boat appeared beside us—two men waving, balancing trays of food with effortless grace.

Lunch had arrived by sea.

Full lobster meals, steaming in the open air, delivered in the middle of the ocean.

I laughed out loud—not because it was extravagant, but because it felt so perfectly Colombian: generous, joyful, and unconcerned with how things were "supposed" to happen.

In that moment, I wasn't reflecting or searching for meaning. I was simply receiving—the sun, the laughter, the abundance of it all.

Because Colombia didn't require stillness like Switzerland. It didn't require surrender like Cairo. What it required—what it offered—was joy without apology. Color without constraint. Story without shame.

For the first time in a long time, I felt like I was allowed to take up space. Not just as a professional. Not just as a woman who had endured or led or built or held it all together. But as a whole person—flawed, vibrant, evolving, alive.

This wasn't about transformation anymore.

It was about embodiment.

The sound of drums still echoed in my ears as I walked back through the old city walls that night. I learned of the significance of the drums. The drums were survival. They were a form of communication. I passed street musicians, couples dancing barefoot, elders nodding from balconies. The city pulsed like a living memory.

And I realized:

I had traveled across continents. Let go of roles, expectations, and weights I didn't even know I was carrying. Felt the breaking. Sat with the silence. Learned to listen—not just to the world, but to myself.

Colombia wasn't the end.

But it reminded me of something essential:

That healing is not only introspection. It's also celebration. It's rhythm. It's color. It's community. It's joy—rooted, embodied, and alive.

The next morning, I sat in the courtyard of the Sofitel Clara, sipping coffee beneath the same arches that once held silence and solitude. The breeze carried the scent of bougainvillea and the hum of a city waking up—not with urgency, but with rhythm. A bell chimed from the old chapel tower, not as a call to worship, but as a reminder: This, too, is sacred.

In that moment, I wasn't reflecting. I wasn't narrating. I wasn't making sense of anything.

I was just there.

Present. Whole. Grateful.

And maybe that's what leadership will look like from now on—not just in how I show up for others, but in how I choose to show up for myself.

With rhythm. With joy. With presence.

Because after all this time, I finally understand:

The journey doesn't end when you return home.

It deepens—once you've remembered who you are.

So now as I prepared to go back home, I realized that I have come full circle. Colombia taught me that transformation is not always quiet or methodical—it can be bold, unapologetic, and bursting with color. In Cartagena's walled city, I saw how the past can live in harmony with the present, how centuries-old walls can hold both reverence and celebration. The Sofitel's journey—from convent, to hospital, to luxury hotel—mirrored my own: transformation without erasure, growth without abandoning history.

But in Palenque, I learned something deeper: that resilience can become a form of joy. Here was a community born from resistance, the first free town in the Americas, where the rhythm of survival became the rhythm of life. Drums echoed not as reminders of struggle, but as affirmations of endurance. The people here didn't just preserve their heritage—they danced it, spoke it, and lived it into the future.

Colombia reminded me that to live fully, you must let your history breathe. You don't have to dismantle the walls you've built for protection; you can open their gates. You can invite music in. You can allow what once felt like survival to become celebration.

By the time I reached Colombia, I realized that each country on my path had given me a piece of the prescription I didn't know I was seeking—Bali's surrender, Japan's intention, Korea's balance, Tanzania's mirror, Ghana's pride, Switzerland's rest, Egypt's integration. But Colombia? Colombia gave me joy. Unfiltered. Unapologetic. Unstoppable. It taught me that transformation is not only about healing what was broken—it is about celebrating what is still alive.

FROM THE FIELD TO THE BOARDROOM

Colombia reminded me that vibrancy is not a distraction from focus—it can be a source of it. Inside the walled city of Cartagena, life moved with an unapologetic energy: music spilling from plazas, street vendors calling out over the scent of fresh arepas, children chasing soccer balls through cobblestone streets. The city didn't try to mute its personality to fit someone else's standard—it led with it.

In the corporate world, leaders often underestimate the power of unapologetic identity. Too often, organizations dilute their uniqueness to appear "professional," stripping away the very qualities that make them magnetic. Cartagena showed me that when culture is lived boldly and visibly, it becomes an irresistible draw—one that fosters loyalty, curiosity, and engagement.

The Sofitel Legend Santa Clara embodied this truth. Its transformation from convent to hospital to hotel didn't erase its history; it layered it. Leaders can do the same with organizations. Reinvention doesn't require erasing what came before—it's about building on it, honoring the strengths of the past while evolving for the future. When change is rooted in respect for what's been, it's easier for people to embrace what's next.

Colombia also revealed a deeper leadership lesson: Joy and performance are not mutually exclusive. In the plazas, business was done over laughter, negotiations happened to the rhythm of music, and connection was as important as the transaction. In companies, when leaders intentionally create environments where energy and authenticity are encouraged, innovation follows. People are more likely to take risks, share ideas, and stay committed when they feel both valued and alive in their work.

The question I brought home from Colombia was this: **How often do we build organizations that people actually want to be part of—not just for the paycheck, but for the pulse of it?** Because when identity is celebrated, history is honored, and joy is woven into the daily rhythm, an organization becomes more than a place to work. It becomes a place to belong.

COLOMBIA:
LEADERSHIP LESSONS IN BOLDNESS AND BELONGING

Boldness invites connection: In Cartagena and Palenque, boldness wasn't just an attitude—it was a way of being. The colors, the music, the unapologetic energy reminded me that when you stand fully in your identity, you draw people in rather than push them away. Leadership isn't about muting your vibrancy to fit a mold—it's about letting your authenticity create its own gravitational pull.

History shapes the present but doesn't define it: Walking through the Sofitel Legend Santa Clara, I felt the presence of every life and purpose that had filled its walls—convent, hospital, hotel. The city itself carried layers of history and resilience, yet refused to be confined by them. Leadership is the same. We carry the architecture of our past, but we choose how to inhabit it today.

Joy is a form of resistance: In Palenque, a community born from escaped slaves, joy wasn't an afterthought—it was central. Music, food, and gatherings weren't just celebrations; they were declarations that life could be abundant despite hardship. In leadership, joy becomes a counterbalance to challenge—a reminder that thriving is as essential as surviving.

- Cultural intelligence requires listening first: Colombia's energy is layered—part celebration, part survival, part reinvention. I learned that to truly appreciate a place, a culture, or a team, you must listen before interpreting. Leadership demands the patience to observe and absorb before acting—to honor the full story, not just your perception of it.

- Expansion requires permission: Colombia reminded me that growth—personal or professional—isn't always about adding more. Sometimes, it's about allowing yourself to take up space with confidence. True expansion begins when you stop asking if you're allowed to lead and start embodying that you belong there. And sometimes, the asking isn't even verbal—it's internal.

PLACES THAT HELD ME IN COLOMBIA

Cartagena's Walled City: Cobblestone streets alive with color, rhythm, and history. Every wall seemed to breathe stories of resilience and reinvention.

Sofitel Legend Santa Clara: Once a convent and hospital, now a sanctuary of quiet elegance where history and renewal coexisted within the same stone walls.

San Basilio de Palenque: The heartbeat of freedom and ancestral pride, where music and laughter carried the legacy of resistance in every drumbeat and dance.

Getsemaní: A neighborhood bursting with murals, music, and unfiltered authenticity—where art was not decoration, but declaration.

Café del Mar: Perched on the old city walls at sunset, overlooking the Caribbean—a reminder that endings, like horizons, can be breathtaking.

Bocagrande: Sleek and modern, its skyline reflected the forward momentum of a city that refuses to be defined by its past alone.

Plaza Santo Domingo: Lively, sun-soaked, where tourists and locals alike gathered under the watchful gaze of Botero's reclining woman—the pulse of joy made visible.

The Caribbean: Vast, warm, and unhurried—a mirror of release and renewal, teaching that sometimes the most powerful movement is flow.

HOTEL
SANTA CLARA

CARTAGENA

Welcome to *Colombia*

PALENQUE

CHAPTER 10

CROSSING BACK:
THE ART OF RETURNING

> " You don't return to
> who you were.
> You return carrying
> who you've become. "

Coming home was supposed to feel like closure. It didn't. Even before I boarded the plane, I knew I wasn't returning to the same life I'd left. There was no desk waiting, no calendar to reclaim, no team to lead. I had already stepped away—from the title, the structure, the identity that had once defined me. What waited now was ... blank.

Not empty—just unwritten.

It felt as if the next chapter of my life were a manuscript waiting for me to fill it. But instead of the pressure to perform, I felt space. Breath. Possibility. I didn't need to hurry toward what was next. I just needed to arrive whole.

The question wasn't *How do I go back?* It was *How do I begin again?*

That question wasn't just about work—it was about voice. For years, I had lived in systems, institutions, and even a marriage that rewarded my silence. I learned that being agreeable, composed, and quietly capable made things easier—for everyone else.

I learned to make myself smaller to preserve peace. To step back when I knew I should step forward. To let others lead, even when the direction felt wrong.

But stillness, I've come to understand, isn't the same as silence. And peace built on suppression isn't peace at all—it's erasure.

This journey showed me that the voice itself was never the problem. Sometimes the truth arrives before the courage to hear it.

Returning home, I knew this much: I would no longer trade my voice for belonging. I could lead differently—not by shrinking, but by standing rooted in what's real.

After decades of running organizations, of moving from one urgent decision to the next, stillness had become my new measure of progress. I no longer needed to be driven by deadlines or deliverables. What I needed was direction—from within.

Each country had left its fingerprint. Bali loosened my grip. Japan taught me rhythm. Korea helped me hold opposites in harmony. Tanzania handed me a mirror. Ghana gave me pride without pretense. Egypt offered courage to be seen. Switzerland, the stillness to rest. And Colombia—the audacity to live boldly.

All of it led here—to this in-between place where endings meet beginnings. The moment after one door closes and before the next one opens.

For much of my career, my value had been tied to productivity—to the visible proof of worth. But now I was learning that creation doesn't always come from motion. Sometimes it comes from pause. From allowing silence to stretch long enough for truth to surface.

There was a time when a blank page would have terrified me. Now, it felt sacred. I had no itinerary, no outcome, no five-year plan. Just a pen and the permission to write something new—not about what I could produce, but about who I could become.

I thought of the shaman in Bali, the fortune slip in Japan, the driver in Tanzania who told me *you're safe*. Each had given me something intangible—a piece of rhythm, a kind of trust. Together, they formed a compass I could follow home.

Coming home, I didn't feel restless. I felt reverent. There was no urgency to rebuild or rebrand. The life I was returning to would be one I designed slowly, with intention—word by word, choice by choice.

I wasn't returning to what I had known. I was returning to myself.

And maybe that's the art of returning—not to resume, but to rewrite.

The journey had taught me how to leave. Now, it was teaching me how to begin.

○

WHAT REMAINS

We don't lead to be seen. We lead to serve something sacred. This journey began with exhaustion. With dissonance. With the quiet realization that I could no longer contort myself to fit the spaces I once believed I had to earn.

But somewhere between the flower offerings of Bali, the stillness of Kyoto, the grit of Seoul, the wide skies of Tanzania, the chaos of Cairo, the clarity of Switzerland, the ancestral pull of Ghana, and the joy still waiting in Colombia—I remembered.

I remembered that leadership is not performance. It is not posture. It is not permission granted by titles or applause.

Leadership is stewardship. It is clarity in complexity. It is care in motion.

And most of all, it is remembering that the truest kind of power is not what you hold—it's what you return to others.

This story may be mine, but it was never just about me. It's about every person who has ever felt too visible and too invisible at once. Every high-achiever who has succeeded their way into disconnection. Every leader who has wondered if there's another way to lead—one with integrity, alignment, and soul.

If there's anything that I can offer up in this journey of mine, it is that:

You are not alone. You are not lost. You are already enough.

The only thing left is to give yourself permission—To lead differently.

ACKNOWLEDGMENTS

This book was written in stillness, but it was not written alone. There are people who walked beside me during the years that led to these pages—some knowingly, others without ever realizing the role they played. Each offered something essential: a question, a challenge, a moment of truth, or the courage to see me more clearly than I could see myself.

I begin with gratitude for Neil Sterrer, my sixth-grade teacher, who dared me long before I understood what that meant. He planted a seed with no expectation of witnessing its bloom—yet he remains here to see the lives shaped by his courage to challenge young minds, mine among them. This book carries the echo of that early permission.

I am grateful to the mentors, colleagues, coaches, leaders, and confidants who trusted me with responsibility, complexity, and moments that demanded more of me than comfort would allow. Even when the lessons were difficult, they shaped my understanding of leadership—and, ultimately, of myself.

To those who walked with me during the seasons of burnout and recalibration: Thank you for your patience, your listening, and your refusal to rush me back into old versions of myself. Your presence without judgment mattered more than advice. Among them was Leslie, who journeyed beside me while courageously navigating her own path of healing and rediscovery after the loss of her father on September 11—her quiet resilience a powerful reminder that stillness can be an act of bravery, and that purpose often emerges when we allow ourselves to slow and listen.

To members of my family and closest friends, thank you for holding space without asking for explanations and allowing me to be vulnerable and human. For your steadiness when I stepped away. For reminding me who I was before achievement became the measure.

I am also grateful to the places that held me during this journey. Across eight countries, I found reflection not in movement alone, but in pause—in unfamiliar landscapes that offered clarity precisely because they asked nothing of me. Life has a way of offering the precise prescription necessary when you are willing to receive it.

Finally, to the reader: Thank you for your willingness to pause, to question, and to consider a different way of leading. If these pages offer you even a fraction of the permission I once received, then this journey has come full circle.

ABOUT THE AUTHOR

Carole M. Adolphe is a senior finance executive, board leader, and transformational strategist with more than three decades of experience spanning government contracting, mergers and acquisitions, and organizational leadership in small to mid-sized organizations. She has served in executive roles as a Chief Financial Officer and Vice President of Contracts, led complex acquisitions and integrations, and advised organizations through periods of growth, disruption, and renewal—including reversing financial declines, shaping strategic pricing decisions, and standing up international operations.

Permission to Lead Differently emerged from a personal reckoning with performance-driven leadership and a global journey across eight countries that reshaped how she understands success, identity, and alignment. Through storytelling and reflection, Carole invites readers to question inherited models of leadership and consider what becomes possible when clarity replaces endurance.

She actively mentors leaders, serves on nonprofit boards, and teaches the next generation of entrepreneurs. Outside of her professional work, Carole finds grounding in travel and long walks through unfamiliar places.